The Harvey Girls

The Harvey Girls

THE WOMEN WHO CIVILIZED THE WEST

Juddi Morris

Walker and Company   New York

First published in the United States of America in 1994 by Walker
Publishing Company, Inc.

Published simultaneously in Canada by Thomas Allen & Son Canada,
Limited, Markham, Ontario

Library of Congress Cataloging-in-Publication Data
Morris, Juddi.
The Harvey girls: the women who civilized the West / by Juddi Morris.
p.   cm.
Includes bibliographical references.
ISBN 0-8027-8302-3.—ISBN 0-8027-8303-1 (reinforced)
1. Southwest, New—History—1848–   2. Southwest, New—Social life
and customs.   3. Waitresses—Southwest, New—History.
4. Restaurants—Southwest, New—History.   5. Fred Harvey (Firm)—
History.   I. Title.
F786.M866   1994
979′.03—dc20   94-2815
CIP

Book design by Claire Naylon Vaccaro

Printed in the United States of America

2   4   6   8   10   9   7   5   3   1

With much love from Mum to Chris. Warm thanks to my editor, Mary Perrotta Rich, and to those Harvey Girls who shared their photographs and memories.

Contents

The
Harvey Girls

1.

Fred Harvey's Dream

*H*istory may credit the U.S. Cavalry, the Winchester rifle, and Sam Colt's pistol with winning the West, but it was the Harvey Girls who civilized it. What in the world brought these young women to a region thought to be "hell on women and horses"?

"Settlements" in the western United States were nothing more than army or trading posts—places where stacks of buffalo hides stank in the heat. Cattle dust, and mud so thick it encrusted the hems of women's dresses, clogged the streets. The population included such unsavory types as gunslingers, striding along wooden sidewalks and through the bat-wing doors of saloons, and drunks, who staggered, passed out, and lay where they fell. After long cattle drives, cowboys rode into town for their first bath in weeks and to sleep in beds and eat meals at a table. Settlements were so far apart that horses were literally ridden to death: It was not unusual for a lathered, foam-flecked animal to drop dead from exhaustion during the ride from one settlement to the next.

The Harvey Girls' story begins as the railroad charged across the West, smoke billowing and cinders flying. Traveling by rail was easier, faster, and less fearsome than traveling by wagon, but it was not easy. Passengers faced many possible dangers—train robberies, locomotive breakdowns, even buffalo herds stampeding across the tracks. But probably the greatest hazard on western lines was the awful food served when the train stopped at eating places during the journey.

During the late nineteenth century, buffalo were slaughtered to the point of near extinction. In Dodge City, Kansas, in 1874, a man sits atop a pile of buffalo hides. *(Kansas State Historical Society)*

Railroad officials gave little thought to the comfort of their passengers; if people were delivered to their destination not too far behind schedule, and in one piece, that was enough. As far as the serving of food was concerned, the railroad business wanted no part of it. The train traveler was therefore at the mercy of station cafés along the way. Most experienced travelers were not as afraid of Indians as they were of contracting an agoniz-

In the 1870s, many of the towns the railroad went through, such as Dodge City, Kansas, had little more than a post office and railroad depot. *(Kansas State Historical Society)*

ing case of food poisoning that would complicate or end their journey, or even kill them.

Fortunately for train passengers, in 1850 a slim, fair-complexioned fif-teen-year-old left his home in London and boarded a sailing ship in Liver-pool. He emigrated to the United States, where he was to change the face of food service across the entire Southwest. As a result, Fred Harvey won the undying gratitude of several generations of hungry travelers and lonely railroad men, sodbusters, and cowhands.

After stepping ashore in New York with only ten dollars in his pocket, Harvey quickly found a two-dollar-a-week job as a "pot walloper" (dish-washer) in an exclusive restaurant. The good-humored boy was a hard worker and soon became a waiter in the elegant establishment.

He began moving west to New Orleans, St. Louis, and on to Kansas, always working in dining houses. He developed an abiding interest in fine food, properly served in pleasant surroundings. When he was not working, he visited other eating houses, dining in the best ones when he had the money. He was eager to see how these establishments ran their businesses.

Harvey also visited their kitchens in off-hours, greeting the chefs and questioning them about the preparation of different dishes. If a chef had the time, he would explain things to the lad, or he might even make a batch of sauce and give pointers on keeping it smooth and free of lumps. Harvey was never happier than when he was learning about the restaurant business.

To pursue his goal of owning a first-class eating place, Harvey took a better-paying job as a traveling freight agent on the Hannibal and St. Joseph Railroad—known as the Horrible and Slow Jolting Line by passengers who had ridden it. The position required constant train travel, but he could now make the money to finance his dream.

On those long trips Harvey took across Kansas, the train stopped at stations during mealtimes. A man would stand on the platform ringing a bell, urging passengers to eat at the railroad café and warning that if they didn't, the cook would throw the food away.

Hungry travelers, pressed for time and fearful of being left behind, bolted from the train and stampeded like a herd of buffalo into the small roadside lunch stands. As Keith L. Bryant, Jr., tells it, there they grabbed "greasy doughnuts and lukewarm, bitter coffee (made once a week); rancid bacon; heavy, cold biscuits called 'sinkers'; bowls of gray stew full of strange looking objects (they hoped were vegetables); antelope steak so tough you couldn't get your fork into the gravy; and worst of all, the dreaded and notorious 'railroad pie': two crusts as tasteless as cardboard, held together by a glue of suspicious looking meat and shrivelled potatoes."[1]

This food was often prepared by a cook who had been trained in a mining or logging camp and had been fired because his cooking was inedible. Service was sloppy, and the surroundings and waitresses were filthy. Passengers elbowed and shoved one another to get served, and then bolted down the awful stuff anywhere they could grab a seat or find a place to stand. Fistfights were often the deciding factor in who would get a chair at the counter.

Standing on the edge of these jostling crowds, Harvey shook his head in disgust, set down the coffee cup holding a vile brew that tasted like ground acorns, and reboarded the train where he sat brooding about the food and manners of these westerners. Sometimes as he stared out the train window, watching the pell-mell rushes into the small roadside lunch stands, he heard the cries of someone who had suffered a disjointed arm or a gouged eyeball trying to get into the café.

Some crooked café owners, in cahoots with railroad crews, played scams on passengers: While still on the train, hungry travelers would pay half a dollar in advance for a meal in the station's restaurant. But the minute the food was placed in front of the diner, the engineer would toot his whistle and the conductor yell "All aboard." The poor traveler, afraid of being left behind in some godforsaken hamlet, would hop up and run for the train, leaving the meal untouched. The food wasn't wasted, however. It was scraped back into the kitchen pots and brought out for the next trainload of victims. The grateful café owners paid the cooperative train crews ten cents a passenger for this caper.

Even if this wasn't the case, meal stops sometimes lasted only a short ten to twenty minutes. It was a well-known fact that the trains didn't dally once the station bell rang and the conductor called "Boaaaaaarrrrd." Passengers were frantic by the time their food arrived and after gulping it down were in worse shape than they had been before eating. They could only hope this food would stay down. It was not unusual for Harvey to help people trying to board the train who were staggering and doubled over in pain with stomach cramps after one of these railroad meals.

"Don't leave me, don't leave me," they would call in hoarse and desperate voices, as the train jerked to a start. As it gathered speed and rolled down the tracks, the cars were filled with the moans of suffering passengers clutching their stomachs and clawing the air in agony.

While the train lurched and swayed across the country, Harvey talked with rich and cosmopolitan foreign visitors to America who were also appalled at this frontier food. The young freight agent could only agree with them. If he were operating his own railroad dining room, he thought, how different it would be run.

Experienced train travelers like Harvey, wary of this railroad food, brought picnic lunches from home. One of these passengers, a correspondent for the *Kansas City Star*, recalls that, "many years ago when you went for a trip on the railroad, somebody at home kindly put up a fried chicken in a shoe-box for you. It was accompanied by a healthy piece of cheese and a varied assortment of hard boiled eggs and some cake. When everybody in the car got out their lunch baskets with the paper covers and the red-bordered napkins, it was an interesting sight . . . the bouquet from those lunches hung around the car all day, and the flies wired ahead for their friends to meet them at the next station."[2]

On the long, slow trip across the scorching prairie, much of this picnic food would spoil before it could be eaten. Maggots hatched in the food, and mice ran up and down the aisles cleaning up any crumbs that were dropped.

Harvey thought just smelling all that rancid food was enough to make you sick to your stomach. Ever the dandy, he wore an immaculate white handkerchief folded into the breast pocket of his suit. As the train jolted

Fred Harvey's dream of high-class restaurants would come true: Note the table settings at the Alvarado Hotel in Albuquerque, New Mexico. *(Kansas State Historical Society)*

down the tracks and flies buzzed against the grimy, fingerprinted train windows and attacked the leftover lunches, Harvey would whip out that snowy handkerchief. He'd place it over his face, take a few deep breaths to settle his heaving stomach, and lean back against the scratchy green train seat and dream of the railroad restaurants he would own.

He planned places as grand as those in New York and New Orleans where he had worked. There would be linen tablecloths from Belfast, the finest crystal from Belgium, heavy English silverware, a varied menu of tasty food, and dark-coated waiters moving quietly around the dining room as they sliced roast beef, flamed crepes at table, and uncorked magnums of champagne nestling in tall, ice-filled silver buckets.

But Harvey did more than dream and complain about the sorry railroad dining conditions; he took action. His experience and imagination told him now was the time. The railroads were young but expanding rapidly; the need for restaurants and hotels would certainly grow with them. If someone could get in early and establish a chain of quality restaurants that catered to travelers' comforts, there would be no limit on how far he could go.

By 1875, in partnership with Jeff P. Rice, Harvey was running two restaurants on the Kansas Pacific Railroad. He and his partner soon fell into heated debate over what the quality of these establishments should be. Whereas Harvey had high standards for the restaurants' food and service, and would never settle for second best, Rice didn't mind cutting a few corners on poor cuts of meat, inferior vegetables, and week-old fruit. With such diametrically opposed views, the two men disagreed constantly. Finally, the quarreling got so bad they decided to split up and sell both places.

Harvey immediately began to shop for another restaurant and railroad to pursue his goal of running a fine eating house. He approached officials at the Burlington line with his ideas on how these railroad dining rooms should be run, but they laughed him out of the boardroom, saying his ideas were far too grand for railroad meals. The man in charge followed him out of the room, still chuckling, but added that he should take those schemes over to the Atchison, Topeka and Santa Fe Railroad, where someone might listen to him. The Santa Fe was a bustling new line and not above putting together some "pretty hare-brained schemes," according to this railroad official.[3]

That's exactly what Harvey did. The Santa Fe was the most rapidly expanding railroad in America under the aggressive leadership of Thomas Nickerson and Charles F. Morse. And it was fast becoming one of the most important lines in the West. Harvey talked to Morse, the general superintendent. A tall gentleman who shared Harvey's taste for fine food, Morse, too, had come up through the ranks as a traveling railroad man and knew about the awful grub served at most of those greasy spoon cafés.

He listened with interest as Harvey talked of depot restaurants, properly run, featuring good food at reasonable prices, served in spotless surroundings. Harvey had so much faith in his ideas, he was able to convince Morse that a profit could be made on such ventures.

Englishman Fred Harvey brought civilized dining to the American West. (*Kansas State Historical Society*)

The terms of Harvey's proposal were as follows: The railroad would provide the building for the restaurant, furnish free freighting of food, ice, coal, water, and transportation for employees. As the café owner, he would supply the equipment for the place, as well as the workers and, of course, the food. Train crews could eat there at half price by using the coupons he would provide.

Harvey continued to sketch his picture of the future, suggesting that fine dining rooms be established in first-class hotels where passengers could stop over and visit the wonderful sights of the Wild West in comfort and luxury. He hoped to transform the nature of railroad meals from torment to pleasure.

Although Morse decided to wait a few years for the hotels, he was willing to begin with a restaurant. So, with a handshake to seal the deal, Harvey was in partnership with this up-and-coming passenger line. His dearest dreams would soon come steaming into the station at Topeka, Kansas, the site of this first cooperative venture with Charlie Morse and the Santa Fe Railroad.

In most business ventures, timing is everything, and Harvey had unknowingly timed his pitch to the railroad perfectly. Tom Nickerson, president of the Santa Fe, and Charlie Morse had recently completed an inspection of railroad facilities up and down the line. On this long trip, the gentlemen had plenty of opportunities to eat at dingy railroad cafés. Like most savvy travelers who were forced to eat the food served in these places, they probably sanitized their digestive systems with a belt of Irish whiskey before eating any of this chow, and after returning to their car, they most likely downed another one for good measure. Still, both men had returned home with uneasy stomachs and an overwhelming desire to do something about the revolting food offered to passengers on their line.

2.
Will They Come?

*a*t the Topeka depot, Harvey bought a dingy, little ten-seat lunch counter with Charlie Morse's backing. Then he rolled up his sleeves and went to work. The place was closed down, scrubbed from wall to wall, and painted in fresh southwestern colors. The floors were refinished, and gleaming gaslight fixtures were installed. Harvey bought glossy Irish linen tablecloths, sparkling crystal, and new silverware; he hired waiters and arranged for the best produce, meat, and other food to be delivered to the back door of the immaculate kitchen.

The restaurant, which was one flight above the street, opened with much fanfare. When patrons ascended the stairs and entered the establishment, they were offered a large, moderately priced menu and received courteous service in handsome surroundings. These qualities would become hallmarks of every Harvey eating house.

Folks raved about the food and the ample portions. For example, a typical English-style breakfast that suited westerners just fine could be bought for thirty-five cents. It consisted of steak and eggs, a large serving of crisp

W aiting for the train at the depot in Topeka, Kansas—home of Harvey's first restaurant. *(Kansas State Historical Society)*

hash brown potatoes, a stack of golden pancakes with pats of fresh butter melting on top and pure maple syrup spilling down the sides. For those with bigger appetites, there was apple pie with coffee for dessert.

The people of Topeka could not believe their town had such a grand place to eat. They found it surprising that Harvey's prices were no higher

M any travelers arranged their schedules to be at a Harvey House at mealtimes. *(Harvey House Museum, Florence, Kansas)*

than those at some hash houses, where it was rumored you could break a tooth on a bowl of oatmeal.

Among the first patrons of the new lunchroom were a group of Plains Indians who came in on a cold and snowy November day, led by the chiefs Spotted Dog, Red Tail, and Fast Bear. It was later reported that Harvey gave them a warm welcome, although the rest of the diners gave them a wide berth. They attracted considerable attention as they ate the fine fare.

The business was an overnight success. Word of the wonderful food spread, and folks flocked to the new lunchroom. In a few weeks the little counter bulged with customers, not only railroad passengers and train crews, but local townsfolk as well. Salesmen, who made up a large number of the railroad's passengers, began to plan their trips so as to be in Topeka at mealtimes. Before long, the new place was so busy that Harvey had to expand the lunchroom. There must be plenty of room to feed the train passengers, he said, and quickly get them on their way again.

Both Harvey and his railroad partner, the Santa Fe, were happy with the situation. Morse was particularly pleased, believing that this excellent eating house was an important factor in pushing the railroad line into the number-one spot in the nation.

Eventually the building was enlarged again, but still more people crowded in for meals. One traveling salesman said, "For a few months it looked as though civilization were going to stop short in her onward march at the capital of Kansas—Topeka, and that the westward course of empire would end at the same spot. Travelers positively declined to go further once they had eaten with Fred Harvey. Traffic backed up, and it became necessary for the Santa Fe to open similar houses at other points along the right of way in order that the West might not be settled in just one spot."[1]

Down the line in a tiny hamlet of Florence, a newly constructed hotel-with-restaurant was having difficulties. The place was rumored to have bedbugs, was underfinanced, and the owner wanted to sell. Morse suggested that Harvey acquire the establishment, refurnish it, and raise its standard of service.

Harvey rode the train down to the little place, looked it over, liked what he saw, and asked the railroad to buy it. At that time the Santa Fe was in a fierce struggle with the Denver and Rio Grande Railroad, with most of its cash involved in that fight, so the directors and Morse could only promise that if Harvey bought the hotel, they would buy it back later. They guaranteed at least two main-line passenger trains would stop for meals each day. This time, a contract was signed with the railroad. "Whatever is fair" was to be the terms between Harvey and the Santa Fe for this contract and all subsequent agreements, and neither party would ever be disappointed.

The building was refurnished in the lavish Harvey manner. Harvey journeyed into Chicago and hired away the head chef from the plush Palmer House restaurant. Rumors began flying around Florence that the cook over at the Harvey House was being paid twice as much as the local banker. Folks gathered on the dusty little street corners and shook their heads in amazement, stunned that any cook could make that much money!

But the European chef from the Windy City, Konrad Allgaier, soon put a stop to all the talk of whether he was "worth it." The Clifton Hotel, as Harvey's newest venture was named, opened on June 14, 1876, and what this expert did with the wild game of the prairies was a delight to the hundreds who dined with him at the place.

Not only were diners happy with Chef Allgaier, so were local hunters and farmers. They were amazed when he offered three and a half dollars for a dozen prairie hens, seventy-five cents for a dozen quail, ten cents a pound for butter, and the highest prices that anybody had heard of for fresh fruit and vegetables.

The novelty of an excellent chef cooking magnificent cuisine in this little backwater burg in Kansas proved irresistible to people. Once again travelers began arranging their schedules to stop at Harvey's restaurants,

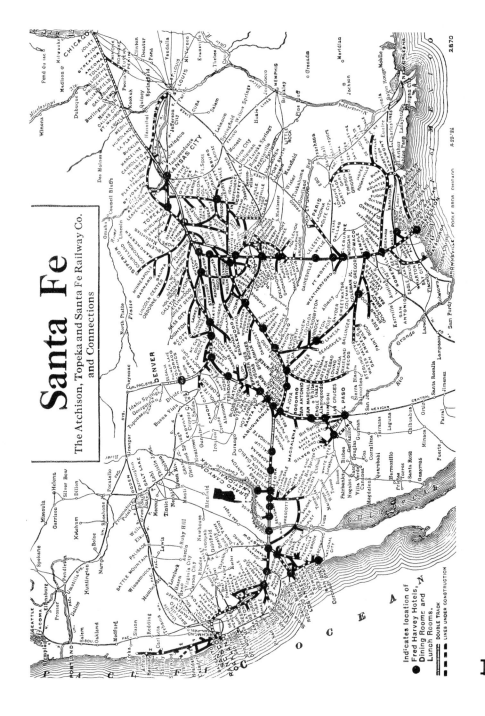

Santa Fe

The Atchison, Topeka and Santa Fe Railway Co. and Connections

Indicates location of Fred Harvey Hotels, Dining Rooms and Lunch Rooms.

DOUBLE TRACK

LINES UNDER CONSTRUCTION

Harvey was quite savvy when he made his deal to be the sole restaurant operator along the route of the Santa Fe Railroad—look how the Santa Fe expanded! (*Kansas State Historical Society*) which were now being referred to as Harvey Houses. Meals at the Florence Harvey House became famous far and wide.

At this time many foreign visitors were touring the United States and were astonished that a little spot like Florence, Kansas, would have a cosmopolitan dining house attached to a first-class hotel. Those who spoke at length with Harvey were also amazed at some of the things he said. "One evening, I shared a cigar and a tot of brandy with the innkeeper," wrote a fellow Englishman. "Harvey said when he first came out to these parts, 'there wasn't a square meal or a decent lodging west of St. Louis, that there were no ladies west of Dodge City and no women west of Albuquerque.' Darned if I don't believe him."[2]

Within a few years, as tracks were laid west, with the cooperation of the Santa Fe, Harvey Houses sprang up at such stops as Hutchinson and Dodge City, Kansas; Las Vegas, Albuquerque, and Gallup, New Mexico; as well as Needles and Barstow, California. By 1884 there were seventeen Harvey Houses along the route of the Santa Fe.

Thanks to Harvey, the Santa Fe was the only line in the West where people could get decent food. As a consequence, its passenger traffic boomed. In 1889, eleven years after opening the Florence dining room, Harvey signed his second contract with the Santa Fe. This time he made a pretty canny deal, obtaining the exclusive right to operate all eating houses along the Santa Fe line.

The Harvey Houses were running smoothly—at least when Harvey could get good waiters. The problem seemed to be that these men of the old West got "liquored up" and didn't come to work, or worse, came to work drunk and bleary-eyed or hung over and shaky. They dropped or threw dishes, made rude remarks to customers, and picked fights. While riding the train from one town to the next, inspecting his dining rooms, Harvey spent many hours worrying about the poor help situation and what could be done about it. Why couldn't he get decent help, he wondered, when he paid well and treated his help fairly?

On one of his surprise visits to the Harvey House in Raton, New Mexico, he found a real mess. A bunch of drunk waiters had gotten into a midnight brawl and had a knife fight. Several of the men had been pretty well carved up and were unable to work. Those who were still on their feet started throwing the restaurant dishes, tables, and chairs at the wall. They pulled plates off the shelves and counters, and when they had wrecked the place, staggered over to the Painted Daisy Saloon for a few more drinks.

By the time a furious Harvey strode into the restaurant, some of the guilty were still sleeping it off on the floor of the kitchen. It is reported that he promptly fired every one of the surly waiters and the stunned manager as well, telling him that he was tired of these men treating customers as if they were in a sleazy hash joint instead of a Harvey House. The waiters shambled off down the street, and Harvey locked the door behind them.

A new manager was approached about taking the job. A recent arrival in town, Tom Gable said he would take it if Harvey would hire waitresses. "Women," he said, "didn't get drunk and have knife fights like men did."[3]

Harvey, desperate for help, agreed, since bad waiters seemed to be the only problem in his eating houses. If it wasn't a knife fight, it was a shooting or a drunken brawl. Even when these men were sober, they were often rude. Some seemed to be afraid of soap and water, while others grew bushy, disagreeable-looking beards. The thought of trim, tidy, and sober waitresses sounded like a dandy idea to Harvey. Gable was hired.

Years later, Gable told a newspaper reporter about his idea of waitresses. "Women were used in eating houses in the east and they proved to be very satisfactory, so I suggested we do the same. Harvey agreed, and that," said Gable, modestly, "is how I brought civilization to New Mexico. The Harvey Girls were the first respectable women those cowboys and miners had ever seen, that is, outside of their own wives and mothers. Those roughnecks learned manners."[4]

This idea, most folks said, was the best one either man ever had. It made Fred Harvey famous, and it assured Tom Gable of a place in the Harvey Corporation for as long as he wanted.

On the train trip back to Topeka after firing the waiters, Harvey gave a lot of thought to how and where he might get women to work in his restaurants. He knew that the West didn't have many working women and that most of them were hardly the kind to be employed in first-class eating houses. He certainly couldn't use the dance hall girls of the saloons, the prostitutes, or the sloppy and ill-mannered serving help used in other eating places. Where, he wondered, as he gazed out the train window at a herd of buffalo raising dust across the countryside, could he find the kind of workers needed?

Once Harvey decided to do something, he was quick to dive into action. When he started his restaurants, he had gone to great lengths to get the finest furniture, the best table linen, the heaviest silver, and the best chefs available. A perfectionist, he was willing to pay for the best, and nothing was too much trouble or too expensive for his businesses. He gave the same kind of painstaking thought to this problem of finding waitresses. He realized his successful string of dining rooms would fail if he could not get good help.

As he got off the train back in Topeka, he thanked the conductor for a good trip, tipped the porter for his services, and stepped down the train steps deep in thought. He couldn't think of even one woman who would be willing to work in these isolated towns, at least not one that he would hire. Where were these waitresses to come from?

At work the next morning, after a good night's sleep, the solution came to him. He put on his hat, left the office, and hurried across the street to the telegraph office. There he sent the following ad, to be put in eastern newspapers: "WANTED—young women, 18 to 30 years of age, of good moral character, attractive and intelligent, as waitresses in Harvey Eating Houses on the Santa Fe Railroad in the West. Wages $17.50 per month with room and board. Liberal tips customary. Experience not necessary. Write Fred Harvey, Union Depot, Kansas City, Missouri."[5]

Folks in this little western town scoffed when they heard his plan, saying the kind of women Harvey wanted would never work as waitresses. They would not come to these frontier, railroad settlements filled with saloons, cattle, prostitutes, and outlaws. Young single women were not about to leave the safety of their homes in the East, one local preacher told Harvey.

In their Sunday morning sermons, ministers talked in hushed and foreboding tones about this crazy scheme. They warned that women who might dare to come would ruin their reputations and could end up in a bordello as scarlet women, or worse yet, fall into the hands of white slavers. The women of the congregation shook their bonneted heads in fright, and the men tightened their lips in disapproval.

Harvey ignored these dire prophecies, kept sending out ads, and sat back to see what would happen. Would the young women come?

3.
Learning the Harvey Way

ou bet they came.

After Harvey ran the series of newspaper ads in eastern news-papers, he set up an employment agency in Chicago to interview applicants. He was determined to get well-educated women who had good manners and a neat and attractive appearance. He wasn't concerned about experience; it might even be a handicap, since they would have to learn the "Harvey way."

If accepted, a woman boarded the Santa Fe and headed west to begin the training some claimed was more difficult than army boot camp. She usually had only about twenty-four hours to pack her bags and tell her family good-bye.

Each woman signed a contract for twelve, nine, or six months, agreeing to learn the "Harvey way" (an expression she would hear over and over, grow tired of, and finally use herself). Furthermore, she agreed to follow all instructions, obey employee rules, go wherever she was assigned to work, and to not marry during the term of the contract. If she married during this time, she would forfeit half her pay, as well as the railroad pass that allowed her to ride free on the Santa Fe line.

The train trip to that first job was paid for by the railroad and served as the first step in learning how to be a Harvey Girl. It was first-class all the way. No sitting up all night in a coach car for prospective Harvey employees; they rode in style in Pullman sleeping cars. Many of these young women had never traveled by train and were amazed at the tricky upper and lower berths the porters made into little beds for sleeping.

All along the way the new trainees ate at Harvey Houses. About an hour before mealtimes and a number of miles from the next restaurant, the conductor, pen and paper in hand, circulated from car to car to announce the next stop and take reservations indicating the number of people to expect in the Harvey House dining room or at the lunch counter. Passengers gave their food choices, and the conductor wired the information ahead to the restaurant. A mile or so from the depot, the engineer blew the train's whistle to alert the restaurant staff of the train's arrival.

By the time the travelers had gotten off the train and followed the porter (banging on a shining brass gong), the first course of salad or fruit was already on the table. Harvey Girls stood quietly near the tables they were assigned to serve as diners were seated.

When the prospective Harvey Girls sat down to eat, they got their first taste of what their own work would be like. They watched with big eyes and growing excitement as the busy waitresses served meals in a pleasant and efficient manner in the relaxed comfort of a dining room.

The trainees were intrigued by the Harvey uniform and stared at the bustling workers, dressed in fresh black dresses with black bow ties under white collars. Trim but comfortable black shoes and stockings peeked from under their swiftly moving skirts. A crisp white pinafore and a white hair ribbon completed the outfit, dazzling the soon-to-be Harvey Girls, as well as the lonely and homesick hearts of many a western male.

Eager passengers crowd into the Casa del Desierto Harvey House in Barstow, California. *(Mojave River Valley Museum, Hazel Poe Hallock Collection)*

When the young women finally reached their training destination and were fitted for uniforms, they were put on duty full-time, assigned to follow, observe, and assist more experienced Harvey Girls.

Topeka was chosen for training because it was a busy railroad town. Most residents worked for the line or had families who did. In fact, nearly everyone in town gathered at the depot each day to see the trains come in, and many stayed over to have a cup of coffee or a meal in the Harvey House.

These Santa Fe people were understanding and gave the new and inexperienced waitresses encouragement, overlooking any mistakes they might make in serving. After all, they were railroad people, and railroad folks claimed to be family.

The training period of thirty days was intense and nerve-racking: There was so much to learn! Pay did not start until training was finished, but most of the women managed fine without money since food and lodging in Harvey dormitories were free. Besides, they were busy during the day and were too tired to go anywhere at night.

Those first weeks were a time of great change for these women, what with the pressure of feeding trainloads of people in a limited amount of time, learning Harvey's code of behavior toward diners, and understanding all the serving rules that were rigidly enforced. This schooling weeded out the weak, timid, and inflexible, as well as those unwilling to work hard.

Opal Sells, who worked for Harvey from 1924 to 1969, had an unnerving experience on one of her first days of training in Amarillo, Texas. As a new trainee, she was so nervous that anything would startle her. On this particular day, she was standing at the counter during a slow time when no trains were in the station. Suddenly, from out of nowhere, a mouse ran across the counter and scampered up her arm. Opal hated mice, so she screamed and climbed on top of the counter. About that time the manager came in and found her perched up there. He looked at her with raised eyebrows. She was so surprised by the appearance of the mouse and the manager that she didn't say a word. She crawled down and headed for the dorm to change her uniform, since she was sure that she'd be fired. The manager sent someone after her. When she had calmed down, she put on her uniform again and went back to work.

As the travelers tucked into their first course, a waitress would take their entrée and drink orders. Soon a drink girl arrived and poured each person's choice: coffee, iced tea, hot tea, or milk. The eager eaters were dumbfounded. How did she know what they wanted to drink? She hadn't asked.

No one had noticed that the waitress who took their orders had moved their cups. A cup right side up in the saucer meant coffee; upside down, hot tea; upside down and tilted against the saucer, iced tea; upside down and off the saucer, milk. Usually the system worked—unless some fidgety diner began moving the cups around. Learning "the cup code" was a small but important part of the training since it made for faster, smoother service in feeding trainloads of passengers.

After the travelers had been served the first course, the manager dramatically entered the dining room with a huge tray of sizzling meat for the entrées balanced on the flat of his hand, and held high above his head. The Harvey Girls gathered swiftly around him as he carved and portioned it out so that each entrée arrived in front of the diners savory and hot.

Ample portions were always given, but the waitresses circulated in the dining room with more platters and dishes, offering second helpings. A serving of roast beef was sliced half as thick as a man's fist, unless the diner preferred a daintier portion. Pies were cut into four pieces instead of the usual six. So generous was Harvey with food that his dying words to his sons who would inherit the restaurant empire were reported to be: "Don't cut the ham too thin, boys."[1]

No Harvey patron ever complained of food monotony. Whatever the entrée was at lunch or dinner, it was not the same one served to passengers yesterday or on the next day's train ride. Menus were sent out from Harvey headquarters for four days at a time, so that if roast beef had been the main dish the first day out, something else would be offered on each of the next three days.

The women were always busy. If there wasn't a train in the station, they were cleaning and spiffing up the dining room. The mahogany counters, chrome-plated coffee urns, crystal glassware, and pastry cases all had to be polished. Alice Meyers White, who with her sister, Bernice Meyers Glenn, became a Harvey Girl in 1932, remembers that she used to dread Saturdays,

Dinner

Blue Points on Shell

English Pea, au Gritton

Filet of Whitefish, Maderia Sauce.
Potato Francaise

Young Capon, Hollandaise Sauce.

Roast Sirloin of Beef, au Jus.   Pork, with Apple Sauce.
Turkey, Stuffed, Cranberry Sauce

Mashed Potatoes.   Boiled Sweet Potatoes.   Elgin Sugar Corn
Marrowfat Peas.   Asparagus Cream Sauce.

Salmi of Duck, Queen Olives.
Baked Veal Pie, English Style.
Charlotte of Peaches Cognac Sauce.

Prairie Chicken, Currant Jelly

Sugar-Cured Ham.   Pickled Lamb s Tongue
Lobster Salad, au Mayonnaise

Celery.   Beets.   French Slaw

Apple Pie   Mince Pie
Cold Custard, a la Chantilly.

New York Ice Cream.   Assorted Cakes.   Bananas
Oranges.   Catawba Wine Jelly   Grapes

Edam and Roquefort Cheese.
Bent's Water Crackers.   French Coffee

Meals, 75 Cents.

WEDNESDAY, NOVEMBER 14, 1888.

Harvey House menus (Kansas State Historical Society; Arizona Department Library, Archives and Public Records)

Fred Harvey

SANTA FE LUNCH ROOM SERVICE

Ripe or Green Olives 20c

Melon Cocktail 20

Cream of New Peas Aux Croutons 15   Consomme Clear 15

PLATE DINNER
Price of Entree Determines Cost of Dinner

Melon Cocktail

Cream of New Peas Aux Croutons	Consomme Clear
Fried Young Chicken, Country Gravy	75
Minute Sirloin Steak, Mushroom Sauce	75
Chef's Special Combination Grill on Toast	80
Breaded Veal Cutlets, Cream Sauce	75
Assorted Cold Dutch Lunch, Potato Salad with Egg	65
Baked Vienna Meat Loaf, Poulette of June Peas	60
Ham Omelette or Cheese Omelette	60

Minced Browned Potatoes   Buttered Beets

Sliced Tomatoes, French Dressing

Choice of Cobbler, Pie, Sherbet or Ice Cream

Bread and Butter

Coffee	Tea	Milk	Cocoa

1. Hungarian Goulash with Vegetables, Mashed Potatoes
   Bread and Butter, Drinks   45
2. Steamed Hamburger Loaf, Demi Glace, Persillade Potatoes
   Bread and Butter, Drinks   45
3. Brains and Scrambled Eggs on Toast, Minced Browned Potatoes
   Bread and Butter, Drinks   45
4. Hot Veal Loaf Sandwich, Mashed Potatoes and Gravy. Drinks 40

Chili Con Carne y Frijoles 20

VEGETABLES

Buttered Beets 10   New Corn on the Cob 10

Minced Browned Potatoes 15   Persillade Potatoes 15

DESSERTS

Pies: Apple, Apricot and Orange Meringue 15

Vanilla or Peppermint Ice Cream 15   Pineapple Sherbet 10

Apple Cobbler 15   Iced Watermelon 20

PREPARED TO ORDER

Veal Cutlet 55   Liver and Bacon 50   Lamb or Pork Chops 60

Tenderloin Steak 1.00   Round Steak 65   Loin End Steak 90

Bacon or Ham and Eggs 50   Omelettes— Cheese or Jelly 45

PLATE SALAD

Head Lettuce 15 Combination 20 Sliced Tomatoes 25 Cottage Cheese 15

Shrimp 40 Chicken 45 Potato 15 Cold Slaw 15

DRINKS

Coffee 10c   Milk 10c   Tea, pot 15c   Buttermilk 10c   Cocoa, pot 15c

Las Vegas N. M.   June. 28 1936   Efton L. Lindsey, Mgr

BEER, ALE AND SANDWICH LIST ON OTHER SIDE

FOR MINERAL WATER, ETC., SEE OTHER SIDE

because that was the day they had to polish all the silver. "It seemed as if everything in the dining room was silver or had some silver on it. In later years when I was married, my husband wanted to buy me a big silver service, but I said, 'No, I never want to polish a piece of silver again as long as I live,' but that was about the only thing I disliked about my job."[2]

Pearl Chandler Ramsey left her home and family in Missouri in 1923 to do her training in San Marcial, New Mexico. She soon learned that

Harvey Girls spent hour after hour not only polishing silver but folding napkins as well. "We never used paper napkins, and those heavily starched linen dinner napkins had to be folded just right, so they would stand up," she recalls.[3]

If a Harvey Girl had nothing else to do, she was expected to dust the premises. Some restaurant managers even put on white gloves and ran their hands along surfaces looking for dust. It took hours to keep the dining rooms spotless in

Alice Meyers, 1937. (Alice Meyers White)

little towns with unpaved streets; dust was stirred up by horses, wagons, and herds of cattle.

"In the summer we fought clouds of dust, and in the winter it was the mud that clung to shoes like glue," explains Ruby Douglas Kuntz, who worked in a New Mexico Harvey House in the late 1920s and 1930s. "Those cowboys would come stomping into the lunch counter with mud caked all over their boots. The busboys used to hate to see them comin', because that meant they'd be scrubbing the floors three times a day trying to stay ahead of all that caked mud. Other places just gave up, but not the Harvey Houses; we always had clean, polished floors."[4]

Each waitress had to keep her station, or the area for which she was responsible, up to standard, and that meant putting away everything that had been used after the patrons left. Tables, chairs, countertops, salt and pepper shakers, and coffee urns were to be spotless, ready for the next diners. Woe unto the waitress who left her work undone.

The manager wasn't the only one checking for dust or dirt. Even more important, Fred Harvey himself might get the notion to do an unexpected inspection of his restaurants along the line. Sometimes he would use the manager's white-glove trick, whipping out that folded white handkerchief from his breast pocket and running it across the shelves behind a counter. If a place was not clean or if something else turned out to be amiss, look out, heads would roll! There'd be trouble for everyone working there, from the manager down to the busboys.

Harvey was adamant about small things, and no gum chewing was one of them. Legend has it that a Harvey Girl was caught chewing gum by the "big cheese" on an unexpected inspection and was fired on the spot for "chewing her cud like a cow." She was hustled aboard the next train for home that same evening.

Harvey's reactions could be violent at times. He might yank the table linen and all the dishes off a table if the cloth was not smoothly ironed or the table not properly set in the Harvey manner: plates an equal distance from the table's edge, the heavy silverware placed just so, water glasses exactly the same distance from the knives, and the napkins folded precisely. The sight of a chipped dish or a wilted bouquet could send him into a towering rage.

Harvey Girls stand ready and waiting for the next train's arrival. *(University of Arizona, Fred Harvey Special Collection)*

Since the blistering heat made passengers thirsty, silver pitchers of ice water, sweating and beaded with the cold, were required on all tables. If Harvey found melted ice, lukewarm water, or smudges on the pitchers, he didn't mind pouring the contents on the floor.

Witnessing one of these tablecloth-yanking or water-pouring scenes was usually enough for the staff to keep things up to snuff until Harvey's next drop-in visit.

Legend has it that friendly train personnel, seeing Harvey on board, would wire ahead in a secret code to warn the employees at the next restaurant that Harvey was rolling their way. The telegram might be worded, "Big cheese to be delivered to Topeka during the dinner hour," or, "Big wind blowing into Albuquerque after breakfast," or maybe, "Winslow, Arizona, expect large sack of potatoes with lunch crowd." On receiving this word, the staff started to scurry around in double time. So when Harvey's train came clacking into the station, he usually found a spotless restaurant and fresh but nervous Harvey Girls waiting with smiling faces.[5]

Railroad people loved to tell of the time that Harvey came home early from a European tour and hit the rails to do an inspection. He was eager to see if the quality of his restaurants had slipped while he was abroad. But he was thwarted by a station master in Topeka who saw him and wired ahead, "Big brass just arrived from Europe, due your station Thursday."[6] The Harvey Girls were ready for him.

If things were in good order, he was quick to congratulate and lavish compliments on every one of the staff. But when his well-known rules were broken, Harvey never hesitated to take action. He was known to be strict but fair. According to the Harvey Girls, if you did your job well, there was no better boss in the world.

The waitresses were required to have the same well-groomed look the restaurants had. Their dress, hairstyle, and makeup were the same whether they worked in New Mexico, California, or Kansas. No variations were per-

ith their crisp, clean uniforms, these 1905 Harvey Girls were a welcome sight to travelers. *(Arizona Department Library, Archives and Public Records)*

mitted. A train passenger of that time remarked on their appearance: "My first Harvey House meal was in the Chicago depot, and I especially noticed the attractive uniforms the Harvey Girls were wearing. It never varied the rest of the trip to Los Angeles. At every stop they wore the same uniforms and looked just as neat and tidy as those at the last one. Finally, the third day, I felt like I knew those girls even though it was a different restaurant, hundreds of miles from that first one in Chicago. You never thought you were slumming when you ate at Harvey Houses, they were class establishments, even in the oddest little places, largely, I think, because the girls were so spunky and special. Most of them could have succeeded at anything they tried to do."[7]

A spill on a uniform meant an immediate change of clothes—even if it left only a tiny spot. Each waitress was given several uniforms but never had to wash them. All laundry, including the restaurant linen, was sent by train to Newton, Kansas, or Needles, California, and returned starched and spotless a couple of days later on the same train. The plant in Newton alone washed four million pieces a year for the Harvey Houses. Bernice Meyers Glenn, who began her career as a Harvey Girl in 1932, remembers that if she worked a split shift, she started out in a fresh uniform each time. "We had all the clean uniforms we wanted without a word from anyone. That was a real incentive for good grooming. We never had to wash our clothes or clean our rooms; that was done for us."[8]

By the time the women had finished this intensive training, they knew "the Harvey way." More important, they knew they were the ones who kept up the standards of the finest eating places in the West.

4.
Who Were Those
Harvey Girls?

*I*n the nineteenth century, women had few options for jobs. They could teach school, clerk in a grocery or dime store, work in a factory, or become a dressmaker or a servant. In the East and Midwest, there were many more women than men, so husbands were even harder to find than jobs. Harvey's ad was a breath of fresh air to many single young women. Here was a way out. It led west, along the railroad, following the wagon ruts and cattle dust of the Santa Fe Trail.

The journey to this new part of the country came at a time when independence and spunk were not qualities appreciated in women. The western adventure, with its excitement and danger, was supposed to be for men. Women were expected to stay close to the family hearth, marry, rear children, and leave things like adventure and excitement to the "menfolk."

As a result, the places the Harvey Girls were headed for had few women:

some schoolteachers, married women, prostitutes, servants, and dance hall girls. And most of the eastern women who came to the West lived within the protection of their families.

Becoming a Harvey Girl gave a woman the chance to leave her past behind and begin a new life. Under Harvey's protective wing, she could change jobs easily and safely, sure of a place to live. She could usually choose where she wanted to work, and if a place wasn't to her liking, she could leave in six months and try another. A woman could work from Kansas to California under the banner of the Harvey Corporation.

Ruby Douglas Kuntz recalls that she was one Harvey Girl who would not consider getting married until she had experienced some travel and excitement. "I traveled all over New Mexico and Arizona— almost any town I wanted to try had a Harvey House, and I could usually find a job at any one of them because I learned to be a good waitress

Ruby Douglas Kuntz in front of the Vaughn, New Mexico, Harvey House in 1938. (*Ruby Douglas Kuntz*)

and was pleasant to the customers and the people I worked with. I was always a 'volunteer.' If the manager wanted somebody to stay late, do extra work, or go to some other Harvey House to serve at a big dinner or banquet, I had my hand up, ready to do it. No, I was too busy making a success of my job and enjoying myself to think too much about marriage, but when the right man came along, I knew and we got married."[1]

And what about the other Harvey Girls? Why did they take such an unorthodox job? Some, frankly, did come aboard to find husbands; some came for adventure; but for the most part, they came for economic reasons. A great many were farmers' daughters or young women from small towns whose families had many children to feed and were struggling to make a living. A few of their fathers were tenant farmers who rented land, scraping a bare living from the soil. The children of the family worked right alongside their father, and if anything happened to the mules, they pulled the plow, too.

Most of these women were grateful for the chance to be hired by Harvey rather than work as a servant or at some other job that paid a pittance. Bertha Spears, a farmer's daughter who began her Harvey House career in 1932, says that she never saved much as a Harvey Girl. Most of what she earned went back to her family, who were struggling on the farm. Not only did she send them money, she spent her vacations working on the farm— putting in longer hours than she did at the Harvey House in Winslow, Arizona. She reports that working for the Harvey Corporation gave her confidence she never had as a farm girl. When she first left her family, Bertha says, she was so timid she dreaded walking down the street past a group of people. A few years later, she was a poised professional who enjoyed talking to people from all walks of life.

She wasn't the only Harvey Girl who helped out on the farm back home. Harvey set up a system that made it possible for farmers' daughters to go home to help with work during the summer and at harvest time. Their jobs at the restaurant were temporarily filled by schoolteachers who were free for the summer and wanted to make extra money.

Opal Sells, also the daughter of a farmer, never expected to become a Harvey Girl. As the youngest child of west Texas pioneers, she stayed on the farm to care for her invalid mother after the other children left home. Following her mother's death, a rich uncle sent Opal to business school. She found a job in Little Rock, Arkansas, as secretary to a businessman, but there her problems began. Her boss was a married man who wanted Opal to become his mistress. The plucky Opal quit her job rather than sit on the man's lap!

In checking the Help Wanted sections of the newspapers, Opal saw the Harvey ad. "People told me not to apply for a waitress job. 'You'll be at the bottom,' they said. But I had heard of the Harvey Girls, about the great food, about all the girls going west from back east. So I went in to see a manager at the Harvey House in Amarillo. He said to me, 'You're the first girl who has walked in here today who wasn't chewing gum. You look like our type.' He hired me the next day and I began work the next morning. I was real nervous. They had such a reputation. You started out right from the beginning. No nail polish, no gum, skirts a certain length from the floor and obeying the rules in the dormitory. People said it was degrading work in a restaurant. Not so in Fred Harvey's."[2]

It wasn't unusual for several generations of a family to work for the Harvey Corporation. Take the Klenke family, for example. The first to start was Henry, the oldest son, who joined the organization in 1887. At seventeen, he was hired as a yardman and pantry boy in a Harvey House in New Mexico. He was thrifty and saved enough money to return to Kansas, marry, have a family, and buy his own farm.

Years later, his oldest daughter, Katie, became a Harvey Girl after her husband died in the flu epidemic of 1918, leaving her with a four-year-old son to support. She and her younger sister, Mary, decided to go to work in a Kansas Harvey House. Their father took them on the train to Hutchinson to the Bisonte Hotel, where the girls were hired and fitted out in uniforms the very same day.

The next sister in line, Josephine, joined her sisters at the age of fourteen to become one of the youngest Harvey Girls. The last sister, Johanna, a sixteen-year-old, also became a Harvey Girl. At the Harvey Houses these sisters had a safe and structured life with plenty of opportunities for advancement if they wanted them.

Johanna remembers, "Leaving that farm and going to work at Dodge City [Kansas] was as exciting as living in New York City for me."[3]

Other women had to overcome their parents' disapproval to become Harvey Girls. People were frightened to think of their daughters going out to the rough and tumble West, with its wild buffaloes and equally wild dance hall girls. Some fathers even went to the Harvey headquarters to make sure their daughters would be working for a reputable company. Most families, however, were soon delighted by the change for the better in these women after only a few months in Harvey's employ.

As Ruby Douglas Kuntz declares, "Being a Harvey Girl gave you a lot of poise. You couldn't go through all that training, work with customers who were used to the very best, and stay ill at ease. It either made you or broke you."[4]

Because of the racist attitudes of the time, African-American women were not hired, and until World War II, few Mexican-American women worked for the Harvey Corporation. Immigrant women were hired, though, which gave them more opportunities than they had elsewhere. In those days, immigrants usually had to take the worst-paying and most difficult and demeaning jobs on the market. They worked in positions that other women were unwilling to accept. But at Harvey Houses they were given the same jobs as other women—jobs that paid well.

Elizabeth Alice Garnas, a Yugoslavian girl whose father was a coal miner in New Mexico, had to go to work in 1926 after her father lost his arm in a mining accident. In Albuquerque, she found work as a maid. Luckily, her employer was a former Harvey Girl who told Elizabeth that she would have a brighter future with the Harvey Corporation. So the young woman applied for and was given a job in the dusty little town of Vaughn, New Mexico. Elizabeth says that she learned to enjoy the town so much that she passed up several opportunities to go to California as a Harvey Girl.

Another Harvey Girl, Ellen Mae Hunt, attended business school in Missouri to become a secretary, but there was almost no secretarial work in her home state in 1922. She saw Harvey's ad and thought that a job with his company would offer plenty of adventure and excitement. She and a friend in Kansas City decided to head west to seek their fortunes. As she recalls: "My friend and I were interviewed by a Miss Steel and we were both hired. We were twenty-one years old and had no idea what we were getting into. We were put on a train the next day and sent to Gallup, New Mexico, for training. I had never seen anything like it; there were saloons on every street. I had never even seen whiskey—Kansas City was dry—and I'd never seen anyone drunk. That was quite an adjustment. I was scared at first, but it didn't take long before both of us loved working for Harvey."[5]

In college towns, students often went to work at Harvey Houses, arranging their schedules so they could attend classes. Two such towns were Las Vegas, home of New Mexico Highlands University, and Albuquerque, site of the University of New Mexico. It proved difficult to work as a Harvey Girl, study, and attend classes all at the same time, but for some students that was the only way to get an education.

The two Meyers sisters grew up on a ranch their father homesteaded not far from Las Vegas, New Mexico. Alice and Bernice knew they could go to college only by working, so they took jobs at the Castañeda Harvey House in 1932. The manager liked them, was impressed that they were determined to go to school, and gave them part-time jobs. They were hard workers

Alice and Bernice Meyers, 1937.
(Alice Meyers White)

with merry hearts and soon became favorites of the patrons. Their tips at the Castañeda were large enough to pay for their schoolbooks, while their salaries paid the tuition at the University of New Mexico.

Alice says that at first, "because of my age—16 or 17—Mr. Lindsay, the manager, questioned my working there, but he reconsidered when he found out I only wanted part-time work and would be attending college. He was listed as my guardian, and my grades were sent to him."[6]

During vacation, the sisters worked at special dinners, banquets, and events at Harvey Houses in larger towns up and down the line. Tips at those functions were big, and Bernice remembers that one night she made thirty-one dollars, which paid for her books for a semester.

When they served banquets in other towns, they enjoyed hopping on the train after their last class of the day and steaming down the tracks to the next Harvey House, clean uniforms and polished work shoes in their bags. This look-alike pair with auburn hair might giggle all the way to work, but they were considered fine and serious workers on the job and the manager was always glad to see them.

"It was during the Depression, and my folks had absolutely no money for board and college tuition for two daughters. Working part-time was the only way we could do it," Bernice says. "But you know, I always felt that training as a Harvey Girl was as important as my college education. I learned about getting along with people, about hard work and carrying my share of the load. The discipline at the Harvey House carried over into my schoolwork, and I was able to juggle everything. We were a congenial bunch there, and the Harvey Corporation treated us like family.

"My parents always stressed the importance of a good education and had a lot of respect for teachers. It was considered a fine job for women, so when I finished school, I quit the Harvey House to teach. I could hardly wait to start, but I was disappointed; it wasn't half as exciting as working at the Castañeda, with all those interesting people coming and going. I missed it."[7]

Alice worked a shift that served the early morning train. "My alarm clock would go off the minute I hit the bed, it seemed like, and off I would go out of the dorm, into the restaurant, sleepy, but you can be sure I was well groomed. I was instantly alert the minute I opened the door to the dining room—you had to be.

"When I was new at work, my job was to prepare poached eggs for anyone who ordered them at my station. Oh, Lord, it was awful; if you broke the yolk or got a speck of shell, you had to start over. The first morning I poached three eggs before I got one right. By the time I served it to the young man who had been sitting there for thirty minutes, I was so nervous my hands were shaking. He was sweet about it, but he was nearly late getting to work. That would have been awful, though, because he was the railroad timekeeper and the trains ran on time or else! I made him many more poached eggs. I married him."[8]

In the 1930s, Jean Begley Bluestein, another student at the University of New Mexico, nearly got blackballed from her campus sorority over her job. "One person on the board," she says, "was appalled that the Chi Omegas had pledged a waitress, and they wondered if I wouldn't quit and get another type of work. I just took my pledge pin off and offered it back. They said, 'Keep your pin,' and I stayed in. Later I took some of the most prestigious girls in the sorority with me to the Grand Canyon to work summers as Harvey Girls."[9]

In the summer of 1959, another college student, Dorothy Pier, a Marquette University junior, worked as a Harvey Girl at luxurious El Tovar Hotel at the Grand Canyon. She says, "I learned about the difference between Europeans and Americans when one European tourist graciously told me, 'You speak very well for a serving girl.' Serving girl, indeed; I was almost a college graduate, but I learned the most from the other waitresses. They taught me how to pick up a tray, carry it, and set it down. They taught me not to wipe grease on my uniform. . . . Like mothers with an eight-year-old daughter, they taught me how to properly tie the bow of my apron.

"They invited me along to hear the ranger's talks under the stars. One even took me with her to Flagstaff on our day off. We attended the Indian powwow, then went to lunch, where we enjoyed professionally evaluating the waitresses.

"What could have been a very lonely day for me, hundreds of miles from home, surrounded by strangers, they made special by baking a cake complete with twenty-one candles—a very memorable twenty-first birthday."[10]

Thus, farmers' daughters, adventurers, immigrants, college students, and young widows all worked together. They came from every part of the United States and from Europe, but they had a common bond: They were Harvey Girls who took pride in their skilled and professional work.

5.
Hear That Whistle Blow

*a*fter training, new waitresses were usually sent to a less desirable location where the restaurants and the tips were smaller and where there wasn't much of a social life. Women with more seniority could choose where they wanted to work, provided there was an opening.

A new employee started at the least important station in the lunchroom and worked her way into better positions in the dining room. Working hard and learning job-related skills were the deciding factors in the move up.

Some Harvey Houses assigned the waitresses badges with numbers on them as a work incentive. Higher numbers went to the newer employees, and numbers were subtracted for the neatest uniform, for extra helpfulness, and for especially pleasant behavior. One exceptionally hardworking beginner went from badge number fourteen to number one in just a year. Some managers even gave the best-groomed employee of the month a large box of chocolates.

Women worked hard to become a "wagon boss," or head waitress. The job carried a great deal of prestige, the pay was better, and a head waitress got a special uniform and a private room in the dormitory. It was a position that called for competence, tact, efficiency, and leadership abilities. No small part of the job was motivating and keeping the Harvey Girls happy. Most new employees loved and respected their first wagon boss for all the motherly guidance given during those first scary days on the job.

One wagon boss who worked for thirty years at the Harvey House in Las Vegas, New Mexico, knew so many people by name and was so well liked, people said she was one of the two most popular women in the state.

Joanne Thompson, a widow with a young daughter, went to work for the Harvey Corporation in 1916 and worked there until 1948. She not only became a head waitress but in a few years was appointed a Harvey House

La Fonda Hotel in Santa Fe, New Mexico, was one of the Harvey Girls' most choice assignments. (University of Arizona, Fred Harvey Special Collection)

Even the lunch counters were kept impeccably neat in preparation for the next wave of customers, Winslow, Arizona, 1910. *(Arizona Department Library, Archives and Public Records)*

manager. She has fond memories of her job: "It was unusual for a woman to be a manager, but I loved it—managing the entire house, hiring, firing, buying food, everything. I relieved a manager and that's how it started. I was never a Harvey Girl again, unless someone needed temporary help. I was sent wherever the head office needed me: Guthrie, Canadian, Topeka,

Amarillo, Slaton, Clovis, San Bernardino, Galveston, Dodge City. It was wonderful. I put my daughter through college that way.

"I took care of the girls. They were like my family, my daughters. Some were very young—one lied and was only fourteen—they would get homesick and I'd arrange to get them a pass home. After a few weeks home, they'd be back, anxious to work again. The Harvey Girls were very happy women."[1]

Restaurant managers were highly paid and earned a lot of respect from fellow Harvey employees, as well as from people of the town. They usually moved every two years until they earned seniority and were sent to the better restaurants along the line. The work was demanding because it meant overseeing every part of the restaurant from the account books to the

Casa del Desierto manager Eddie Behean and family in front of a Harvey House in Barstow, California, 1931. *(Mojave River Valley Museum, Addie Bassett Collection)*

kitchen staff, but the managers were well compensated and given the best housing and furnished maid service. Paid annual vacations with train and meal passes, as well as free lodging at Harvey Houses along the way, came with the job, too.

C. Bristol, assistant general manager of the Santa Fe Railroad, was impressed by the performance of a restaurant manager in La Junta after severe floods washed out bridges and rails in Colorado. In a letter to the superintendent of the Harvey Corporation, Bristol wrote: "Mr. Lesser had, as you know, a big crowd to feed three times a day and at a time when there was no way to get supplies into La Junta from any direction he provided fine meals. He took hold of the situation so that he got nothing but the highest praise from all of the stranded passengers. When things got monotonous and time was dragging heavily upon them, he wheeled a Victrola into the lobby, cleared out the chairs and tables and they had music and dancing as long as they wanted it. It kept down many a complaint and they all seemed to be having a good time."[2]

By the late 1880s, with the help of the railroad, Harvey House restaurants were established every hundred miles along the Santa Fe, making the line famous. It was selling more tickets than any other railroad moving west. Everybody wanted to ride the Santa Fe trains and dine on the superb food served by the Harvey Girls. What had been a harrowing journey was beginning to seem more like a picnic. It was probably during this time that "Meals by Fred Harvey" became the slogan of this up-and-coming railroad line.

With the focus on the exquisite meals, it stood to reason that the chef was at the top of the hierarchy at the Harvey Houses. Harvey hired the best-qualified men he could find, and if he had an especially fine meal in a restaurant somewhere, he didn't mind going through the swinging doors into the kitchen to try hiring away the genius presiding over the roaring stove. Harvey encouraged creativity among his chefs by putting their best dishes on the menu up and down the line at all of his dining rooms.

One Italian chef, Victor Vizetti, had charge of several Harvey dining rooms in Arizona. Once he found himself without a chef either in Williams or in Winslow, so he cooked lunch there, jumped on another train back to cook dinner in Williams, and returned to Winslow just in time to prepare dinner there. He was in Williams to do a midnight supper for passengers on a late train and charged back to Winslow to prepare breakfast the next morning.

The Harvey Girls treated the chefs with due respect, jollying them out of bad moods, flirting with them in the good ones, and humoring their temper

The kitchen crew at the Vaughn, New Mexico, Harvey House. *(Mojave River Valley Museum, Addie Bassett Collection)*

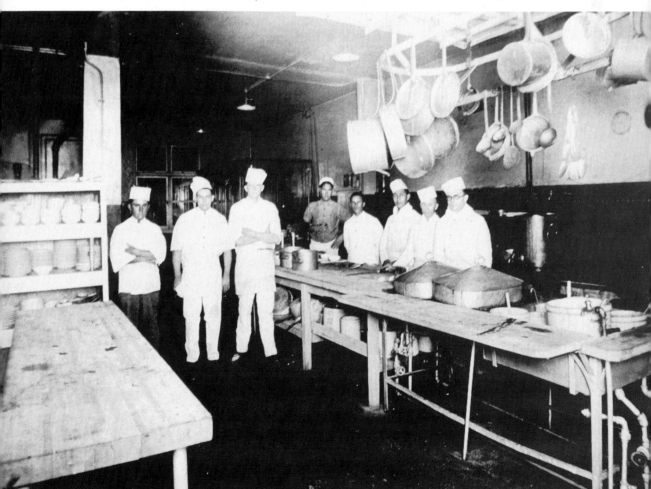

HARVEY EMPLOYEES - LAS VEGAS, N.MEX. JULY 14, 1936 OOOR PHOTO

In 1936, the Harvey staff at the Castañeda Hotel, Las Vegas, New Mexico, included bell hops, dishwashers, two head waitresses, a cook, house mother, manager, day clerk, night clerk, baker, and many others who made the House run smoothly. (Alice Meyers White)

tantrums. Chefs made large salaries, were well respected in the community, and were given paid vacations. They and their immediate families had a train and meal pass to ride anywhere the Santa Fe went. Many of the Harvey Girls married men from the Harvey House kitchens.

Even in a tiny town, a large staff of workers was required to run a Harvey House. For that was the only way to feed trainloads of passengers quickly and send them on their way. A restaurant consisting of a lunchroom and a dining room had a manager, a chef with several assistants, a head waitress, at least thirty Harvey Girls, a baker, a butcher, pantry girls, and busboys. The population of one of these little towns would double as soon as Harvey's staff moved in. If a hotel was established as well, the population might even triple. Not only did Fred Harvey civilize this part of the country, but he also helped populate it with a new breed of working woman who did much to change the rough reputation of towns smelling of cattle and full of dusty-faced men wearing boots and revolvers.

Harvey Girls and kitchen staff bustle about so Santa Fe passengers are served promptly. *(University of Arizona, Fred Harvey Special Collection)*

Canadian, Texas, was a good example of a rowdy cattle town that sported a Harvey House. Set in hundreds of miles of open prairie and prime cattle land, it was a rancher's paradise and an important railhead where thousands of cattle were driven to be shipped east.

The Harvey House was the finest building in Canadian. It was two stories high and made of brick. Covered archways connected it to the depot, and on a hot day the breeze blew through the walkway, making it a pleasant spot. On warm nights, after passengers on the last train had been fed, the Harvey Girls would pull chairs outside and sit drinking iced tea until it was time for the dorm door to close. When they had time off, they would sit there in the shade sewing, reading, or writing letters home. According to Ruby Douglas Kuntz, "Until you've lived in one of those hot dry places you have no idea how much shade meant. Since the West wasn't humid like the East, if you could get out of that parching sun, you could get cool."[3]

Two to four passenger trains stopped every day. One of the duties of a busboy at the Gainesville Harvey House was to spot the incoming trains and alert the chef and the rest of the staff. He would stand out on the platform where he could see for miles up the tracks. At the first glimpse of the puffing engine, he would run back, report to the chef, then seize a big brass gong and whack the daylights out of it.

Everything was ready when the passengers arrived. In the next half hour the staff of the restaurant served eighty or more customers from the train in approximately thirty minutes without rushing them, thanks to split-second teamwork and efficiency. While people were eating, the manager would pass through the dining room calmly saying that passengers would be given ample notice before the train's departure. Then a few minutes later, he went through again, reassuring passengers that they still had ten minutes.

Clara Quartier, who worked for Fred Harvey in several towns in Oklahoma and Arizona during the 1930s, remembers that the staff moved quickly but quietly when serving. "You could hear a pin drop in a Harvey House

A Harvey Girl at the all-important coffee urn. *(University of Arizona, Fred Harvey Special Collection)*

dining room," she stated. "All sterling, dishes, china, and everything else was carried on trays by us girls. You could be fired for carrying even a water glass in your hand."[4]

Although travelers didn't have too much extra time to linger over coffee, the Harvey Houses were famous for the fine brew they served. As Johanna Klenke, who worked as a Harvey Girl until 1930, recalls: "That coffee—folks always raved about how wonderful it was. We had strict rules on how to prepare it. The coffee never stayed in the urns longer than two hours. If we sold only one cup at the end of that time, we threw it out and started again. It was never stale or had that boiled taste. A silver coffee- or teapot sat at every table, and diners could refill their cups anytime. I was always astonished at how much coffee people

Ruthanna Walz, 1938. (*Ruthanna Walz Caster*)

could drink. We never refilled a coffee cup; we always threw out what was left and poured in fresh coffee."[5]

Another menu favorite was the fresh, crisp salad with Thousand Island dressing—it tasted so good in that hot, dusty country. "The dressing was poured over a crisp quarter-head of lettuce to each guest," says Ruthanna Walz Caster, who began work at La Fonda Hotel in New Mexico in 1936.[6] So many people asked what was in the salad dressing that the recipe was printed on little cards and handed to anyone who asked. Thoughtful gestures like that created much goodwill for the restaurants.

The menu also featured freshly squeezed California orange juice. If a manager found a pitcher of orange juice waiting in the refrigerator, there was trouble. The juice had to be squeezed fresh on order and served in a good-sized glass resting on a bed of crushed ice.

Customers at Harvey Houses knew they were eating a special meal and wanted to present a neat appearance. Cowboys got ready by shining their boots, railroaders would comb their hair, and grizzled prospectors washed their clothes and made a trip to the barbership. Although coats were compulsory at the linen-covered tables in the dining room, no one was ever turned away. A man arriving in his shirtsleeves could wear one of the alpaca jackets kept in the coat room for this express purpose. Or, if he preferred, he could take his meal in the lunchroom.

In addition to these paying customers among the townspeople and train passengers, those who could not afford the price of a meal often ate at the Harvey Houses.

This practice was especially common during the Great Depression of the 1930s when whole families, coming out of the Dust Bowl, rode empty freight cars to California in search of work. When the train stopped, these people came to the back door of the Harvey Houses and asked for food. They were usually fed without charge.

During that time, Bob O'Sullivan, his mother, and his sister were driving west to meet Sullivan's father, who had found work in California. Because money was supposed to be waiting for them in Albuquerque, they had left home in Chicago without enough funds for the entire trip. But when they reached the New Mexico town, the money was not waiting. So there they were, their old car loaded to the roof, stuck in New Mexico.

In an article that appeared in the *Chicago Tribune* many years later, Sullivan wrote about this experience.

It was hot and dusty and late afternoon as my sister and I waited for my mother to come out of the Albuquerque Railway Express office.

When she did, she was very upset. She stopped on the steps of the loading dock for a few seconds, wiped her eyes, came to the car and got in. . . .

When I asked if we could get something to eat, she didn't answer for a moment. Then she said, "Of course we can. We have to, don't we?"

She drove about two blocks along the railroad tracks to the Harvey House Restaurant and took us inside. . . .

When a waitress came over to show us to a table, Mother took her a few feet away from my sister and me and spoke to her in a low voice. The waitress listened and then went to the kitchen. She came back with a man who was wearing a dark suit.

He and my mother talked for a few more minutes. He nodded and led us all to a table where he pulled out a chair and seated my mother. . . .

"What would you like?" the waitress asked.

"Perhaps sandwiches for the children," my mother said, "and I'd like a cup of coffee." The girl was starting to write it down when the man put his hand over her order book.

"Why don't you let me order for you?" he said. Then not waiting for an answer from my mother, he told the girl we would all start with hot soup and then we'd have the beef stew, mashed potatoes, bread and butter and coffee for the lady. He asked my sister and me if we wanted milk or hot chocolate.

We both said, "Yes, sir."

"Milk and hot chocolate for the children and some of the cobbler all around and these people are the guests of Fred Harvey."

I saw my mother say, "Thank you," but I didn't hear her voice.

When the last of the cobbler was gone and we rose to leave, my mother pushed a couple of coins toward the waitress. The girl pushed them back with a smile.

"Oh, no ma'am. You're Mr. Harvey's guests," she said and placed two bags in front of my mother.

"The manager said I was to wrap up what you didn't eat, so you could take it along."

In the car my mother and my sister looked in the bags, which clearly contained a greater volume of food than we'd had for dinner.

"What's in them?" I asked.

"Loaves and fishes," she said, "Loaves and fishes."[7]

The Harvey Girls were part of a business that had a heart.

6.
Life in a Harvey House

The Harvey Girls lived in handsome dormitories, two to a room, under the vigilant eye of a house mother. Curfew was at ten o'clock during the week and at twelve o'clock on Saturday night. Special permission could be granted by the chaperon to stay out later for special occasions like dances, but the door was always locked at the regular time. If the matron had to open it for somebody who was late, the young woman's name was written in a tardy book. Missing curfew three times was grounds to be fired.

Strict standards of behavior, moral as well as professional, were expected of Harvey Girls. Young men who had always played fast and loose with women found that these women were a different breed from those at the saloons. If a man wanted to go out with one, he'd better mind his manners, act like a gentleman, and treat a Harvey Girl with respect.

Ruby Douglas Kuntz gives some of the reasons why this was so: "Harvey Girls learned to be self-assured and poised. It was our training. We were well-paid working women, who were proud of our independence. We could travel anywhere the Santa Fe would take us. I wasn't about to go out with some galoot who chewed tobacco, spit on the street, and walked in front of me. We were used to being treated politely. Why, on duty, the wagon boss and the manager wouldn't stand for any rough talk or bad behavior around us girls."[1]

Ruby goes on to tell the story about the night her roommate was late coming into the dormitory.

Her beau had a ranch four miles out of town where he was building a house. One day when she was off work, he and his sister came by and picked her up in a snazzy red buggy, pulled by this beautiful black horse. Oh, what a fancy rig it was! I guess they were just riding around the countryside when they took a notion to go out to see the new house.

Well, they just had a wonderful time driving out there. She said they stopped to target shoot with a twenty-two, then at the bend of a little creek they had a picnic lunch his sis had packed. Finally, they got out to the ranch house and looked around. They were sitting on the front porch steps admiring the view, when she noticed the sun was setting. She panicked, realizing they would never get back to town on time and wondering how in the world would she ever get into the dorm without waking up Mrs. Watkins, our house mother?

She evidently sweated bullets on the way back into town; they all did, and that included the horse, I'm sure. When they pulled up in front of the dorm, she said she looked up and all the windows were dark because it was after eleven o'clock. Of course she just knew her goose was cooked, but she tiptoed around the building and stood under our window. Fortunately it was summer, and the window was open. I was asleep, but I woke up to hear someone calling, "Ruby, Ruby," and then a handful of gravel hit the window screen. I went over to the window, and there was my roommate motioning me to let her in. Well, I felt my way down those stairs, unlocked that big front door, and she came flying into the hall in her bare feet.

We crept up the stairs, one by one, barely breathing, stopping to hold our breath every time one of those darned steps squeaked. When we made it to the top, I breathed a sigh of relief. We crept into the room and after closing the door, fell on our beds, started to giggle, then laughed and we laughed until our sides nearly split. I guess it was the relief after all of that nervous strain.

You can be sure she was never late again. All of us needed our jobs and weren't willing to risk losing them. I guess she felt like she'd used up all her luck that time.

Oh, by the way, she and Bill [her beau] got married in a few months and moved out to the ranch to that adobe house where they lived and raised a family. We had some fine times out there, too.[2]

Most dormitories had a courting parlor where (with the door open) Harvey Girls could visit with gentlemen callers. Otherwise the rule was a strict "no men in the dorm." If a workman or any other authorized male had to climb the stairs to the women's quarters, the house mother would sing out in a loud voice that reverberated up and down the halls, "Man on second floor, girls, man on second." The women would scramble around, pulling on wrappers, covering up hair rolled on curlers, and making themselves generally presentable.

In the evenings they might relax in their rooms or enjoy a game of croquet or take a walk. Sometimes they played the piano, banjo, or ukulele. Some individuals might recite poetry or give readings or act in plays. Many loved to sing and participated in sing-alongs.

Most dorms had a sewing room, too. The Harvey Girls liked to make their own dresses and were among the best-dressed women in town when they were out of uniform. After wearing uniforms all day, they loved to get

Veteran Harvey Girls Effie Aleshire and Hazel Roberts in their room in Barstow, California. *(Mojave River Valley Museum)*

dressed up when they went out. If there was a dance at the Grange Hall, the Harvey Girls could hold their own with any of the town's fanciest dressers. In fact, some of the townswomen used to be jealous of them and envied their clothes.

At Christmastime many Harvey Houses had a party with a tree and all the trimmings. Gifts from the management and a tidy bonus for hard workers were standard practices. Each woman could invite a gentleman guest, and everyone really kicked up their heels. "The Harvey Corporation surely knew how to treat their employees," says Bernice Meyers Glenn. "In many ways, we were treated like privileged family."[3]

Each January, in one small town in Arizona, the dry goods store offered a present to every female customer who had bought more than twenty dollars' worth of goods the preceding year. The Harvey Girls had spending money, so they usually were eligible and came home with new slippers, yardage for new dresses, a snappy hat, or a pair of elbow-length gloves.

In these small communities the Harvey House became the social center of the town. Local ranchers, cowboys, and businessmen used it as a meeting place. The women became acquainted with most people of the town and were considered fine citizens, invited to participate in most church and community events. Alice Meyers White remembers that the railroad and Harvey people were considered the cream of the crop socially. The Harvey Girls were asked to join local women's clubs and other organizations.

Effie Jenks, who worked at the Alvarado Harvey House in the 1920s, describes the hospitality shown to her and the other Harvey Girls. "When I first came to the Alvarado Hotel in Albuquerque, some of the socially prominent families gave parties for the girls. The Mayor and his wife held an open house at New Year's and a prominent dentist's wife gave an annual tea at which her friend, a woman generally considered to be the social leader in Albuquerque, poured. A doctor sometimes took the girls on his rounds making house calls."[4]

Ice-cream socials, with homemade cake and ice cream, were popular, and box suppers took place several times a year. Local women prepared their nicest food, putting it in a decorated box or basket to be auctioned to the highest-bidding man. The winning gentleman then ate supper with the woman whose basket he bought. The Harvey Corporation often furnished the food for any woman who entered these auctions, but it was up to her to make the box look tempting and run up the bidding.

Despite the pleasant social life, some of the Harvey Girls despised these desert towns at first. Accustomed to the tree-covered, eastern part of the country, they couldn't believe their eyes—where were the trees, the shade? They took no notice of trees that had been planted around many of the Harvey Houses, for these were just knee-high sticks covered with green leaves.

Ruthanna Walz Caster was from the fertile farming land of Kansas. "When I arrived at Lamy, New Mexico, in 1936, I was absolutely amazed. It was pure desert—dry and no trees. But you know . . . in no time I was rid of the hay fever that had bothered me so much back in Kansas."[5]

By the time the women had worked long enough to get a vacation and returned home for a visit, they found something strange had happened: They felt hemmed in by all those trees. Their families were surprised at the eagerness with which they boarded the train to go back to those little wind-swept towns.

As the cars clicked west along the tracks, the Harvey Girls realized they had missed those western sunsets that stained the sky purple, red, and pink. They thought of the times when there wasn't a train due, of how they would stroll outside town to watch a full moon come up over the prairie. They missed the smell of the sagebrush during one of those quick summer showers. But most of all, they missed the western people who were so open and ready to be friendly.

Many of the women loved to don trousers, heavy boots, and big old hats, and hike out into the country. Those who enjoyed horseback riding would rent nags from the livery stables and sally forth across the desert for miles. Outdoor physical activities were very popular in these western towns, and the women thoroughly enjoyed them.

When they had the time to do so, they took train trips up and down the line to visit other Harvey Girls and have a meal at their restaurants. They enjoyed these busmen's holidays and liked seeing if things were up to snuff at the other eating houses. If they weren't, they went back and reported, with pride, how much better their own house was.

Many men of the old West loved practical jokes and horseplay and enjoyed teasing the Harvey Girls. One story that has achieved legendary status concerns a railroad brakeman, named Snyder, who got off the train to eat at a Harvey House in Guthrie, Oklahoma. He spied a bunch of frogs jumping around a water tank near the tracks. Catching a few of the little things, he dropped them into his pockets and walked into the restaurant. The waitresses were getting ready for an incoming passenger train, and everything was in order, including cups in place on each table.

Snyder slipped the frogs from his pockets and placed the little creatures into several cups.

Well, the train rolled in, the passengers sat down, and the drink girls started pouring hot coffee into those waiting cups. The frogs struggled to get out, some swimming wildly while others jumped up and down, in and out, splashing liquid everywhere. Those that broke free hopped all over the room, ricocheting off the walls onto the patrons. One even jumped into a lady's handbag; another became tangled in a woman's hair; and a third settled on a woman's hat and began to croak! Pandemonium broke out—women screamed, men cursed, people ran this way and that, and the frogs jumped around the room.

When things settled down and the women passengers stopped shrieking, fresh beverages were served, but most of the passengers refused to drink them and ran for the train.

The manager was furious. He began an investigation, questioning the staff for the next several days, but found no leads. The issue was finally dropped. The frog caper remained a mystery until the culprit confessed many years later. He was still chuckling about it.

Don Eason, a relief chef who worked at Harvey Houses along the line in the 1930s, remembers the fun the employees used to have on their time off. "We played a prank on one of the guys in our dorm. He was the soundest sleeper you can imagine. That guy could sleep through a tornado. One night, a bunch of us carried him, cot and all, down the stairs and set him in front of the depot outside. He never woke up so we just left him. Trains passed that cot all night, but he got a good night's sleep right there. Railroad security guards finally found him in the morning and woke him in time to get dressed for work."[6]

Many of the Harvey Girls who were farmer's daughters were physically strong. And even if they didn't have a rural background, their work kept them in shape. A number of them enjoyed playing on softball teams. In fact, some Harvey Houses had their own teams, which traveled up and down the rails to other towns to compete. Harvey encouraged this pastime and bought handsome uniforms for his players. Even when they were off work and playing sports, the women looked spiffy and attractive.

As much as people enjoyed eating at the Harvey Houses, the waitresses were admired even more than the food they served. One New Mexico male burst into poetry, singing their praise:

> Harvey Houses, don't you savvy;
> clean across the old Mojave
> On the Santa Fe they've strung 'em
> like a string of Indian beads.
> We all couldn't eat without 'em
> but the slickest thing about 'em,
> Is the Harvey skirts that hustle up the feeds.
> I have seen some splendid paintings in my day,
> and I have looked at faultless statuary;
> I have seen the orchard trees a-bloom in May,
> and watched their colors in the shadows vary;

Many a lonely young man was smitten with the Harvey Girls. (*Kansas State Historical Society*)

> I have viewed the noblest shrines in Italy,
> And gazed upon the richest mosques of Turkey—
> But the fairest of all sights, it seems to me,
> Was the Harvey girl I saw in Albuquerque.[7]

Even Will Rogers, the famous movie star, western philosopher, and humorist, joined in the compliments. "In the early days," he said, "the traveler fed on the buffalo. For doing so, the buffalo got his picture on the nickel. Well, Fred Harvey should have his picture on one side of the dime, and one of his waitresses with her arms full of delicious ham and eggs on the other side, 'cause they have kept the West supplied with food and wives."[8]

Although the male Harvey employees may have admired the waitresses, dating between staff members was prohibited. But the women could date railroad men. According to Bernice Meyers Glenn, "The railroad men were fond of Harvey Girls and treated us with a lot of respect. Many of us married them—both my sister and I did. My husband was an engineer, and hers was a railroad timekeeper."[9]

Ruthanna Walz Caster recalls that when she was working at the Castañeda at Las Vegas, New Mexico, she started to date a young university student named Warren who worked part-time as a cook. "We tried to keep it quiet, but Mr. Lindsay, the manager, found out. He hit the ceiling and fired Warren. I always thought it was interesting that he didn't fire me. I guess he just liked me better. I know there was no love lost between the

Ruthanna Walz married Warren Caster on January 8, 1939.

two men. I guess it was worth it to Warren. We've been married for fifty-three years."[10]

Yes, romances bloomed, and more than one house mother complained of running a matrimonial agency. In the latter part of the nineteenth century an estimated five thousand Harvey Girls walked down the aisle with railroad engineers, conductors, station agents, local merchants, ranchers, lawyers, and salesmen.

Harvey always staged parties for the newlyweds and often gave the bride away. He had married in 1859, and he kidded prospective brides who wanted him to escort them, saying that he thanked God he wasn't getting married every time he walked down the aisle with a bride.

Western lore says that more marriages were made in Harvey Houses than in any other institution under *H* except heaven. Many of the firstborn male children of these unions were named Fred or Harvey or both, and you-know-who was the godfather.

These adventurous women became the matriarchs of the West. Lenore Dills, who worked for the Santa Fe, says that "many children and grandchildren of former Harvey Girls boast about their mother or grandmother being a true pioneer, and coming west with the Harvey Houses. It carries a great deal more prestige than coming west in a covered wagon. Anybody could ride in a covered wagon, but only a lady could become a Harvey Girl."[11]

7.
Their Finest Hour

The coming of World War I had little effect on the Harvey Corporation, but the Great Depression closed many of its restaurants. People had no money to travel, so railroads and hotels felt the pinch first. Although people had to eat and have shelter, they didn't *have* to take vacations. Even the formerly rich were beginning to wonder where their next meal was coming from, and previously wealthy stockbrokers were said to be selling apples on street corners in New York City.

As travel ground to a crawl, passenger trains were taken off the rails, so the Harvey Houses had few travelers to feed. Ruby Douglas Kuntz, who was working in a New Mexico House at the time, says that "during the Depression it was really frightening to see so few people on the trains. Gradually fewer and fewer employees were needed to work in the restaurants and were let go. I think they sent all the Harvey House kitchen equipment from our restaurant to larger ones along the line. The day we closed was certainly a sad time for me. A big chunk of my life came to an end when I took off that uniform for the last time. I'll never forget those Harvey days."[1]

Whenever it was possible, members of the Harvey staff were transferred to other restaurants. Managers with years of seniority felt lucky even to be sent to less desirable locations. At least they had a job, they said, and were grateful for that.

It was unnerving to all to see so many people out of work. Railroad employees saw whole families riding in boxcars. They couldn't make a living at home and had been told there were jobs in California. People sold their household goods for nearly nothing and climbed into their old jalopies or onto freight trains with little more than the clothes on their backs.

The restaurants were having a hard time, but they still tried to feed the folks who came to the back door hungry. Most of these weary travelers were pitifully eager to do odd jobs for a meal. Willa Mae Jordan, a schoolteacher who lived next to the railroad tracks in a tiny Texas town, says she'll never be able to forget "those dirty, exhausted, little whey-faced children and the hopeless look in their parents' eyes. It was scary. We all wondered how this could happen in the United States, but it did. We fed everybody we could, but the day finally came when my mother and I had a can of tomatoes and a box of soda crackers in the cupboard, and we didn't know how long that would have to last."[2]

The development of faster trains also contributed to the demise of the Harvey Houses. Trains like the Chief and the Super Chief had dining cars run by the Harvey Corporation. Passengers might be eating a superb four-course meal on board as the train slid through the little town where it used to stop. The few stops the trains did make were shorter, too. Travelers barely had time to descend the steps and walk the length of the train to stretch their legs before the conductor called "All aboard," and they were under way, speeding across the continent.

Harvey House chefs took jobs in the dining cars aboard the trains, but most disliked being away from home. They were often on the road a week at a time, given two days at home, then climbed back onto the train again.

Nevertheless, they were glad to have any kind of job, and to keep working for the Harvey Corporation softened the blow of being away from home.

The start of World War II gave the failing Harvey Houses a giant boost. Railroads were the main form of transportation across the country so the armed forces were moved by rail, swelling passenger travel by more than 600 percent. Many Harvey Houses all but became troop dining rooms for military personnel riding the Santa Fe line. Eating houses that were closed during the Depression or barely tottering along now had more customers than they could handle.

During this time the

Movie star Shirley Temple was a guest of the Santa Fe Railroad on the Super Chief's first run in 1938. *(Ruthanna Walz Caster)*

Santa Fe reported that a million meals were prepared each month between the Harvey Houses and railroad dining cars. Although the company needed the business, this influx of military people lowered the standard of the famous Harvey way. How could the restaurants expect to feed up to two thousand soldiers a day, not to mention packing almost as many box lunches, and continue their quality food and service operation? They tried, but it was impossible.

With so many women working in war-related jobs, it was hard to keep Harvey Girls or to replace those who joined the war effort. The corporation gave up all ideas of having women sign yearly work contracts. As for promising not to marry while employed as a Harvey Girl, that was forgotten, and women of all ages, single, married, or divorced, were welcomed. "That proud corps of women in spotless uniforms, well versed in the proper Harvey manner, gave way to women who would never, ever have been hired in the old days," former chef Don Eason says.[3]

These new employees were taught the rudiments of service as quickly as possible, but the training did not always take. Ray Barbour, the manager of the Harvey House in Chicago's Union Station, tells of noticing a new busboy loading a tray in the dining room, banging and clattering dishes and silver. "I said to him, 'Couldn't you be a little more quiet?' He snarled back, 'You keep your blankety blank nose out of my business, and I'll keep mine out of yours.' Flabbergasted, I walked away. About two hours later the boy approached me and said, 'I'm awfully sorry I was rude to you, Mr. Barbour. I didn't know that you were the manager—I thought you were a customer.' "[4]

The overall quality was slipping, and one day, paper napkins crept onto the tables, replacing the linen ones of the past. One could almost hear the long dead Harvey say in a sad but patriotic voice, "All right, people, the nation is at war, and the troop trains must be fed."

Feed them they did, with the help of inexperienced waitresses—wives, sisters, and mothers of servicemen wanting to do their bit. Even gray-haired Harvey Girls left retirement, struggled back into uniform, and began to feed the boys. Bridget Colson, age seventy, came out of retirement to lend a hand at Ash Fork, Arizona, and the manager reported she did so with the same old-time finesse and efficiency.

Harvey Houses across the country had to rehire many women to meet the demand of the troop trains. Those with experience were sent throughout the West, helping to open restaurants that had been closed. There was so much business—sometimes two trains would come in instead of one. Workers prepared five hundred box lunches at a time for the trains, as well as serving trainloads of men in the restaurants. "It wasn't the Depression that changed the Harvey Houses forever, it was the war," says Don Eason.[5]

Addie Park Basset, a Harvey Girl who worked in Barstow, California, talks about some of her wartime experiences. "At first we tried to give all the boys our usual special Fred Harvey service. We about killed ourselves with over three hundred men to serve. Our good manager, Mr. Krause, would stay up all night trying to get information on the trains so we would have some idea of how many people we would have to feed the next day.

At the Bisonte Hotel in Hutchinson, Kansas, as many as six or eight troop trains a day were fed during World War II. The Bisonte closed on May 31, 1946. *(Mary K. Hoover)*

But so many of the troop movements were secret, and we would find out nothing until they rolled up to the front door. And almost everything was rationed. Well, it didn't take very long to discover we couldn't give our usual Fred Harvey service. A lot of things were changed. We removed all the beautiful linen table cloths, moved our eight, four, and two-seater tables, closed in the front of the verandah, and put in banquet-type tables. That's how we could seat 344 people at one time."[6]

These long banquet tables appeared in every available space at the Harvey Houses, including porches, patios, and cocktail lounges. But sometimes even more seating was required. At Kansas City in the Union Station and at Los Angeles' Union Station, special military dining rooms were established for the use of the troops. And a hotel lobby was filled with tables in Dodge City, Kansas.

Vance Sellers, a young infantryman en route to Italy, wrote his parents that "we are on a train crossing the United States. Yesterday at noon, we ate outside a restaurant in the middle of nowhere. Fortunately, the weather was warm and they had set up long tables outside the restaurant which was already full. Don't worry, Mother, they're feeding us good food even if it's served outside. Makes me remember all those fishing trips down on the Leon River. Well, when this old war is over, that's the first place you'll find me."[7]

A Harvey House staff could get off work at night and be told they were slated to feed five hundred men the next day. When the next day came and went, these exhausted people had served no fewer than twenty-four hundred servicemen!

At a Colorado Harvey House, nineteen members of a local women's club volunteered to serve the troop trains. Students from the Salt City Business College helped employees at Hutchinson, Kansas. In Dodge City, the wives of army engineers pitched in and offered their services. At Winslow, Arizona, the largest military stop on the Santa Fe line, twenty-five women of the town, called Victory Girls, helped as they were needed. Manager Carl

Weber said at that time, "These women may be called at four o'clock in the morning, if necessary. If it were not for them thousands of soldiers, sailors and marines would go hungry, and I presume everyone realizes how hungry a young man gets. With their help, our Harvey House fed 30,000 men during October."[8]

With the exception of the wagon boss and two captains, the entire serving force at Gallup, New Mexico, was composed of Navajo girls from a nearby mission school. They did a fine job, and soldiers from the East were thrilled to meet real Native American Harvey Girls.

Even guests at the Alvarado Hotel in Albuquerque jumped behind counters, picked up serving trays, and began to wait on soldiers as they spilled out of troop trains in waves.

Winslow, Barstow, Needles, and Albuquerque Harvey Houses were major stops for military trains. Here they hired a separate group of waitresses, called "troop train girls," who served only servicemen. These women lived in separate quarters and were on call twenty-four hours a day.

One troop train girl (who does not wish to be named) remembers a poignant encounter during that trying time.

Sometimes, I would go off duty after working twelve or fourteen hours serving those military trains, drag myself up the stairs, wash my face, and drop into bed exhausted, but I couldn't fall asleep. I'd lie there listening to those trains rumbling through the night and think of all the men on board who were scared and lonesome and wondering where they were headed and how soon they would be facing death and the enemy.

One night when I couldn't get to sleep, I slipped on a pair of slacks and a shirt, brushed my hair, and went down the stairs to the kitchen to get a cup of hot chocolate. The chef on duty made it, dropped in two marshmallows and a dollop of whipped cream, patted me on the shoulder, and suggested that I take it outside to one of the benches by the depot and try to relax.

It was a bright moonlight night and so quiet. I sat down on a bench, slipped off my loafers, put my feet up, and rested my chin on my knees. In a minute I heard that lonesome whistle at the Hatch crossing and knew it was a troop train—not one for a meal stop, but one to take on water or use the telegraph office. In a couple of minutes it came down the tracks and began to slide into the station. I just sat there listening to the music of the radio the kitchen crew had on. When the engineer braked to a stop, one of the coach cars was right across from me. I could see men sleeping with their heads back against the seats. They looked so young.

All at once a young dark-haired officer stepped out of the car and came down the steps past me with a large portfolio of papers and went into the telegraph office. A couple of minutes later he came back toward the train. I said hello, and he stopped and lit a cigarette. He said something like what a beautiful night it was, and I agreed. From the kitchen radio came the sounds of "I'll Be Seeing You," that haunting wartime song. I felt tears come into my eyes; the train started to gather steam; he went toward the steps, looked back at me, and said, "Your hair looks so pretty in the moonlight, I think I'm dreaming." "No," I said, "you're not, I'm real and this is Hatch, New Mexico." He touched his fingers to his cap in a small salute, swung up the steps, and said, "I'll be seeing you, New Mexico girl." I never saw him again (that I know of), but I've never forgotten that night. I've had two happy marriages, but I never hear that song but my throat gets tight and tears well up in my eyes.[9]

Like the troop train girls, most people in these small towns dealt willingly with shortages and sacrificed gladly for the war effort. But some local residents, in a less than patriotic mood, were often annoyed that the restaurants were so crowded with soldiers that they, the townspeople, could not get served.

To combat these hard feelings, the Harvey Corporation began an advertising campaign to explain the crowded situation to patrons around the country, using Private Pringle, a composite name for all servicemen. One ad ran as follows: "A tip for a customer? Well, hardly! But there *are* times when we *do* want to express a genuine, 'Thank you' to our guests. For instance: A troop train speeds westward. A sudden change in schedule and dinner must be planned for the next stop—where the Fred Harvey restaurant has just 30 minutes to get ready. Extra help must be mustered, extra food prepared, everything geared like clockwork, to feed husky, hungry fighting men and send them on their way.

"At such times our civilian patrons must forgo the distinctive service they have learned to expect of us. To them we say, 'Thanks for your good humored patience and understanding. You are helping us to carry out our vital wartime assignment!' "[10]

Rationing was also a problem. Sumptuous Harvey meals were no longer possible. Coffee was one of the first scarcities, and only a single cup was poured. Gone were the silver coffeepots on each table steaming with Harvey's fresh and hot roasted brand. Some Harvey Girls, in desperation, now tried to compensate by offering unlimited pats of butter, but soon that too was rationed. Every day seemed to bring more rationed items, but the Harvey Girls muddled through magnificently.

Despite the scarcity of trained help and the problem of rationing, the troops were fed and neither the Harvey Corporation nor its six thousand employees needed to make any apologies for the job they did during World War II. It may have been their finest hour.

8.
The Cavalcade Ends

a traveler, standing at the Santa Fe depot in Las Vegas, New Mexico, one afternoon, looked with interest at a large, impressive building that dwarfed the nearby ticket office. The massive structure was built in the style of the old southwestern missions, with a plastered exterior, wide outside verandahs, and a partly enclosed courtyard. The shadows beginning to invade the courtyard already crept into its empty fountain, but sunlight still struck the central tower and the sign that read, "The Castañeda, 1898."

"At that moment the Santa Fe Chief arrived for its three-minute Las Vegas stop, and two elderly trainmen leaned from the baggage car to answer a question from the stranger on the platform. As the Chief began to move, one trainman said: 'There were more good looking women working there than any place in this town!' The other nodded and called back: 'They served good meals, too.' "[1]

The same nostalgic statements might have been made about all the Harvey Houses across the Southwest.

The Castañeda. *(Alice Meyers White)*

Although World War II gave the failing restaurants new life, after peace was declared they began to falter. The stream of some one hundred thousand Harvey Girls, who had come west at the turn of the century to civilize the dining habits of the public, remained in force and fed the troops during the war, but by 1950 declining business led to the closing of Harvey Houses in one small town after another. Most of the Harvey business was now concentrated in dining cars on the trains, hotels and restaurants in national parks, and in the large cities of California, Arizona, New Mexico, and Illinois. The greatest chain of eating houses the United States had ever known went into a second and final decline because few people were riding passenger trains.

When the Wright brothers made their first flight in a machine called an

Only luxury Harvey Houses, such as the La Fonda in Santa Fe, New Mexico, remained open after the war ended. *(University of Arizona, Fred Harvey Special Collection)*

airplane and Henry Ford set up an automobile assembly line, they started sagas that were to finish mass railroad passenger service. The development of modern aircraft and high-speed automobiles helped to make the trains obsolete.

The use of automobiles for long-distance travel became common. After World War II, plants and factories geared up, turning out cars as efficiently as they had military vehicles. Most families now had an automobile in the garage and were eager to see the rest of the United States in it. One automobile manufacturer's slogan even became "See the USA in your Chevrolet."

In fact, the death in 1901 of Fred Harvey, whose health had been failing for fifteen years, really hadn't changed the hotels and restaurants as greatly as the Great Depression, World War II, and the automobile did. Although the founder was missed by the corporation and his family, service was not disrupted. His sons, Ford and Byron, carried on the old traditions that were already in place and continued with the duties they had assumed when Harvey's health began to fail.

The brothers did, however, set up separate offices to simplify management. Ford, in Kansas City, took charge of the hotels and restaurants, while Byron managed the dining cars out of a Chicago office. At the time of Harvey's death, the chain included fifteen hotels, forty-seven restaurants, thirty railroad dining cars, and food service on the San

An outdoor dining room at the La Fonda (*Ruthanna Walz Caster*)

Francisco Bay ferry system. The company had reached its zenith in 1917 with one hundred Harvey eating houses ranging from Chicago, south to Galveston, Texas, and west to the Pacific coast.

From the 1880s until 1940, the Harvey Girls were the workforce that made Harvey Houses across the country the most successful restaurants of their time. Those who went on to other careers found themselves well prepared: In the restaurants they had learned to work with dignity, cool heads, and warm hearts.

Careers in nursing, teaching, or business often seemed easy or even dull compared to the work in Harvey Houses, where each train brought a new

In 1937 passengers crowded the Santa Fe Plaza, but after World War II, railroad traffic was never the same. (*Ruthanna Walz Caster*)

The Harvey Girls—a most successful group of women! *(Ruthanna Walz Caster)*

group of people, new problems, and new rewards. The women were used to being stretched on the job. They soon learned to be flexible if they were to function in what was for the time a fast-paced existence. Where else could the daughter of a poor farmer or railroader become a head waitress or manager of a first-class restaurant, whose patrons were often the world's richest and best-traveled people?

Olive Winter Loomis, who worked from 1918 to 1940 as a Harvey Girl, says, "I have special memories of all the Harvey Girls. They were special women, doing a special job in lovely places. Whatever you did, everything was done with care. You never forget that. You are always a Harvey Girl, all your life."[2]

Thousands of women found adventure and a new and better way of life in the West. They brought culture and fine cuisine to a raw but beautiful country. Where the grunt and growl of frontier barbarism had held sway, they set forth a law of *please* and *thank you*. The Harvey Girls never built a railroad, shot a buffalo, or escaped an Indian raid, yet they played as big a part in the settling of the West as most men who traveled to this region during the latter half of the nineteenth century.

Before working as Harvey Girls, the future looked bleak to these women, but a desire for something better altered their lives. Fred Harvey gave them a vehicle for this change, but he didn't make them what they were. They were something special to begin with. The Harvey Girls were ahead of their time and pioneered the way west for other working women, riding the rails to a new part of the country where they flourished, living respected and successful lives.

Source Notes

1. Fred Harvey's Dream

1. Keith L. Bryant, Jr., *History of the Atchison, Topeka and Santa Fe Railway* (New York: Macmillan, 1974), p. 107.
2. Robert G. Athern, *Westward the Briton* (Lincoln: University of Nebraska Press, 1953), p. 24.
3. Lucius M. Beebe, "Purveyor to the West," *American Heritage Magazine*, vol. 18, no. 2 (February 1967), p. 28.

2. Will They Come?

1. Beebe, "Purveyor to the West," p. 14.
2. Letter in Fred Harvey files, University of Arizona, Tucson.
3. Erna Fergusson, *Our Southwest* (New York: Knopf, 1940), p. 195.
4. Ibid., p. 196.

5. James D. Henderson, *Meals by Fred Harvey* (Fort Worth: Texas Christian University Press, 1969), p. 20.

3. Learning the Harvey Way

1. Henderson, *Meals by Fred Harvey*, p. 1.
2. Alice Meyers White, interview, May 1992.
3. Dorothy Townsend, "Harvey Girls: How the West Was Won," *Los Angeles Times*, June 27, 1984.
4. Ruby Douglas Kuntz, interview, October 1991.
5. Fred Harvey files, University of Arizona, Tucson.
6. Ibid.
7. Letter from Mrs. George Johnson, in ibid.
8. Bernice Meyers Glenn, interview, May 1992.

4. Who Were Those Harvey Girls?

1. Ruby Douglas Kuntz, interview, October 1991.
2. Leslie Poling-Kempes, *The Harvey Girls* (New York: Paragon House, 1989), p. 76.
3. Johanna Klenke, interview, May 1992.
4. Ruby Douglas Kuntz, interview, October 1991.
5. Poling-Kempes, *The Harvey Girls*, p. 77.
6. Alice Meyers White, interview, May 1992.
7. Bernice Meyers Glenn, interview, May 1992.
8. Alice Meyers White, interview, May 1992.
9. Townsend, "Harvey Girls: How the West Was Won."
10. Dorothy Pier, interview, November 1991.

5. Hear That Whistle Blow

1. Poling-Kempes, *The Harvey Girls*, p. 95.
2. Letter from C. Bristol, Fred Harvey files, University of Arizona, Tucson.
3. Ruby Douglas Kuntz, interview, October 1991.
4. "The Phantom Poet," *Mojave Magazine*, June 1973.
5. Johanna Klenke, interview, May 1992.
6. Ruthanna Walz Caster, interview, April 1992.
7. Bob O'Sullivan, "It's 44 Years Late but Thanks for the Memory, Mr. Harvey," *Chicago Tribune*, December 11, 1988.

6. Life in a Harvey House

1. Ruby Douglas Kuntz, interview, October 1991.
2. Ibid.
3. Bernice Meyers Glenn, interview, May 1992.
4. Poling-Kempes, *The Harvey Girls*, p. 162.
5. Ruthanna Walz Caster, interview, May 1992.
6. Don Eason, interview, November 1991.
7. Henderson, *Meals by Fred Harvey*, p. 31.
8. Clipping from the scrapbook of Opal Sells.
9. Bernice Meyers Glenn, interview, May 1992.
10. Ruthanna Walz Caster, interview, May 1992.
11. Lenore Dils, *Horny Toad Man* (El Paso: Boots and Saddles Press, 1966), p. 66.

7. Their Finest Hour

1. Ruby Douglas Kuntz, interview, May 1992.
2. Willa Mae Jordan, interview, May 1992.
3. Don Eason, interview, November 1991.
4. Fred Harvey files, University of Arizona, Tucson.
5. Don Eason, interview, November 1991.
6. Poling-Kempes, *The Harvey Girls*, pp. 196–97.
7. Letter from Vance Sellers to his parents.
8. Harvey Corporation files, Northern Arizona University, Flagstaff.
9. Harvey Girl who asked not to be identified, interview, September 1991.
10. Brochure in Fred Harvey files, University of Arizona, Tucson.

8. The Cavalcade Ends

1. Henderson, *Meals by Fred Harvey*, p. 1.
2. Townsend, "Harvey Girls: How the West Was Won."

Bibliography

Adams, Samuel Hopkins. *The Harvey Girls*. New York: Random House, 1942.

Athern, Robert G. *Westward the Briton*. Lincoln: University of Nebraska Press, 1953.

Beebe, Lucius M. "Purveyor to the West." *American Heritage Magazine*, vol. 18, no. 2 (February 1967).

Beebe, Lucius M., and Klegg, Charles. *Hear the Train Blow*. New York: Dutton, 1952.

Botkin, B. A., and Harlow, Alvin F. *A Treasury of Folklore*. New York: Crown, 1953.

Bryant, Keith L., Jr. *History of the Atchison, Topeka and Santa Fe Railroad*. New York: Macmillan, 1974.

Clark, Ira G. *Then Came the Railroads*. Norman: University of Oklahoma Press, 1958.

Cox, James A. "How Good Food and Harvey 'Skirts' Won the West." *Smithsonian Magazine*, September 1987.

Day, Donald. *The Autobiography of Will Rogers*. Boston: Houghton Mifflin, 1949.

Dils, Lenore. *Horny Toad Man*. El Paso: Boots and Saddles Press, 1966.

Fergusson, Erna. *Our Southwest*. New York: Knopf, 1940.

Friermood, Elizabeth Hamilton. *One of Fred's Girls*. New York: Doubleday, 1970.

Harvey, Fred. *The Great Southwest Along the Santa Fe*. Tucson: University of Arizona Special Collection. 1911.

———. *The Great Southwest Along the Santa Fe*. Tucson: University of Arizona Collection, 1923.

Henderson, James D. *Meals by Fred Harvey*. Fort Worth: Texas Christian University Press, 1969.

Hildebrand, Kay. "Harvey Girls Long a Part of Kansas City Scene." *Kansas City Star*, February 17, 1946.

Holbrook, Stewart H. *Story of American Railroads*. New York: Crown, 1947.

Hubbard, Elbert. *Eulogy to Fred Harvey*. Fred Harvey files, University of Arizona, Tucson, 1907.

Hurd, Charles W. "The Fred Harvey System." *Colorado Magazine*, July 1949.

Jones, Sam, P. "Writes Sam P. Jones." *Anniston, Alabama Newspaper*, April 1911.

Kelly, Carla. "No More Beans." *American History Illustrated*, June 1981.

Lindbergh, Anne Morrow. *Hour of Gold, Hour of Lead*. New York and London: Harcourt Brace Jovanovich, 1973.

Marshall, James. *Santa Fe: The Railroad That Built an Empire*. New York: Random House, 1945.

Moon, Germaine L. Ramounachou. *Barstow Depot and Harvey Houses*. Barstow, CA: Mojave River Valley Museum Association, 1980.

Mullen, Jack. "America's Best-Fed Travelers." *Santa Fe Magazine*, December 1943.

O'Sullivan, Bob. "It's 44 Years Late but Thanks for the Memory, Mr. Harvey." *Chicago Tribune*, December 11, 1988.

"The Phantom Poet." *Mojave Magazine*, June 1973.

Poling-Kempes, Leslie. *The Harvey Girls*. New York: Paragon House, 1989.

Thomas, Diane. *The Southwestern Detours*. Phoenix: Hunter Publishing, 1978.

Townsend, Dorothy. "Harvey Girls: How the West Was Won." *Los Angeles Times*, June 27, 1984.

Waters, L. L. *Steel Trails to Santa Fe*. Lawrence: University of Kansas Press, 1950.

Index